Creative Approaches for Counseling Individual Children in the School Setting

by Diane S. Senn, Ed.S.

YouthLight, Inc.
Chapin, SC 29036

Cover Design by Amy Rule
Layout / Graphics by Amy Rule
Project Editing by Susan Bowman

ISBN 1-59850-011-2

Library of Congress Number
2005938408

10 9 8 7 6 5 4 3
Printed in the United States

Acknowledgements:

A SPECIAL THANK YOU TO THE FOLLOWING:

To my friend and fellow counselor, Betts Gatewood, for giving her time and effort to read, give feedback, and edit each page of the book. Thanks for your willingness and support you have given.

To Bob and Susan Bowman, presidents of YouthLight, Incorporated, for their support, wisdom, encouragement, time given to review and edit, and their belief in this project.

To Amy Rule, graphic designer, for her friendliness, promptness, creativity, and her professional ability to bring "life" to the pages.

To my husband, Stan, for his support, love, and patience. And to my children, Bryan and Lindsay, for their understanding and encouragement to keep writing. Thank you for sharing your time.

To my parents, Armand and Junell Shealy, who with their unconditional love and support have guided me through the years. Thank you for your wisdom.

And most importantly we give honor and thanks to God, our guiding light.

Table of Contents:

WHY INDIVIDUAL COUNSELING IN SCHOOLS?

Individual school counseling is a component of the Developmental Guidance and Counseling Program. Individual counseling, in our delivery system, is a responsive service in which we seek to meet the students' immediate needs and concerns. As school counselors our role is to help address issues and concerns that may negatively affect the students' personal, social, and/or academic-career development. If personal concerns, difficulties dealing with relationships, and difficulties with normal developmental tasks occur, these can interfere with the student's development and success.

Individual counseling offers needed support to guide the child through a problem area. There is a wide variance in the purpose of individual counseling in order to meet the various needs of the child. The needs of each child can vary from:

- an outlet to talk/vent in order to think things through,
- to the benefit received from a caring counselor/child friendship,
- to the support shared in dealing with a difficult situation that the child cannot change,
- to the assistance given to the child in creating a plan for things they can change,
- to help in strengthening needed skills for success.

In individual counseling we deal with:

- building trust with the student so he/she feels comfortable venting negative feelings and exploring ways to deal effectively with those negative feelings.
- learning and implementing problem solving steps.
- teaching, practicing, and assisting the student in implementing appropriate social skills to enhance his/her interpersonal relationships.
- providing extra attention to facilitate self-respect and confidence.
- developing coping skills to deal with difficult and/or unchangeable life events.
- helping the student look at or think about problems in a different way that will not negatively affect his/her school work/social relationships.
- assisting the child to review his/her behavior choices and the consequences of those choices.
- designing and assisting in implementation of behavior plans for targeted behaviors.
- and providing support for academic skills – motivation, organization skills, helpful hints in using their learning strengths, etc.

Individual counseling in the school setting is typically short term in nature. School counselors do not provide therapy and when necessary, referrals are made to outside agencies.

Introduction:

WHAT IS INVOLVED IN INDIVIDUAL COUNSELING?

Individual school counseling involves meeting/counseling with the student to help deal with and work through a problem that is bothering the student and/or adversely affecting the student's learning. Assessment of and working through the problem with a child sometimes can be accomplished by verbal communication, however, the elementary child may have difficulty expressing him/her self or difficulty pinpointing what is bothering him/her. Therefore, at the elementary level, creative counseling strategies and forms of play may be utilized to assess and to deal with the problem. The individual counseling activities shared in this book pull from various theories, techniques, and different modalities. The following list specifies various techniques that are shared in this book:

- use of play
- games
- incomplete sentences
- metaphors
- questions
- rating scales
- re-framing
- storytelling
- dialoguing
- music
- use of puppets
- object lessons
- role playing
- journaling
- checklist
- self-monitoring
- pictures
- drawing
- clay
- worksheets
- role reversal
- cognitive restructuring
- behavioral contracts
- **biblio-counseling** – only a few children's books are referenced in these materials however I feel that the use of children's books can be a vital part of counseling. Books can diminish fears and connect children to others who have similar worries and concerns. Children's books are a wonderful source to extend advice, techniques, and support. New books are added everyday. I encourage you to continue to review and utilize children's books in the counseling process.

These techniques are pulled from many different theories. In counseling we connect with the child, determine their needs, and target the problem area. Then we select the activities/techniques that are most appropriate in helping the child and the problem. In order to do this it is important that we have an understanding of the different theories and the intent of their techniques. Below highlights only a few theories:

Cognitive Counseling – The focus of this approach is on changing negative thoughts to more positive and constructive thinking.

Behavioral Counseling – This approach involves a relearning process of reinforcing helpful behaviors while eliminating unhelpful or maladaptive behaviors.

Person-Centered Counseling – The counselor uses facilitative responses as the child shares about the problem.

Play Counseling – This approach allows the child to express his/her feelings and work out the problem through play. Play becomes the language of the child.

Eclectic Counseling – This approach involves a blend of counseling approaches depending on the needs of the child and the problem.

I encourage us to be knowledgeable of the various counseling theories and to continue updating ourselves on the different theories and techniques.

HOW DO YOU USE THIS BOOK?

FIRST: You need to **connect** with the child. Get to know the student's likes, interests, strengths, etc. Establish rapport, empathy, acceptance and trust. See activities in the "Getting to Know...The Person and the Problem" in the INFORMATION GATHERING section.

SECOND: **Gather information** about the student and his/her needs. Listen to the student, consult and collaborate with significant adults in the student's life, and utilize formal and informal inventories to determine strengths, weaknesses, needs, etc.
See INFORMATION GATHERING section.

THIRD: **Explore** the problem. Gain insight into the student's thoughts and feelings.
See UNDERSTANDING AND DEALING WITH THE PROBLEM Section.

FOURTH: Together **create** and **implement** a plan. As you are selecting strategies / approaches / activities to help the student, keep in mind their style and interest as well as your own style and interest as a counselor. There is never one set method to address a need for there are too many variables involved, such as: the child, their temperament, their cognitive level, their interest, their likes and dislikes, etc. as well as what you as a counselor have the ability and enjoy doing. If you as a counselor do not "enjoy" doing a specific activity then chances are it will not be a success for the student. Address the needs of the student by selecting appropriate activities from the seven topic area sections of: FEELINGS, SELF-CONCEPT, FRIENDSHIP, ACADEMIC SUPPORT, BEHAVOR, DIVORCE, and DEATH.

FIFTH: **Assess** if the "plan" is working. Ask yourself, the student, and others involved if the counseling plan is making a difference. If not, revise.

Forms are shared in the FORMS section to facilitate students connecting with the counseling (referral forms and appointment notices), to collaborate with the significant adults in the child's life (feedback form), and a form to create an individual counseling plan for documentation of contacts, summary information, and formulating a plan.

Confidentiality

As stated in the American School Counselor Association Ethical Standards for School Counselors: "Each person has the right to privacy and thereby the right to expect the counselor-counselee relationship to comply with all laws, policies, and ethical standards pertaining to confidentiality." (p. 121 The ASCA National Model) The laws require us to disclose information in order to prevent clear and imminent danger to the counselee and others. In regards to confidentiality review the law, your own district policies, and our ethical standards.

We need to respect the student's right to privacy, however there are times in the counseling process when significant others need to be involved in the counseling process, to have knowledge of the problem and knowledge about the plan to effect change. Involving the child in the decision-making process of who else to involve and what can be shared maintains respect for their privacy while including the support of others.

Support Systems

I encourage you to take advantage of a student's support system - the parent, teacher, and other significant adults. Be knowledgeable of, include, and involve others so all can be unified to effect change for the child. As needs unfold for the student, encourage him/her to choose others in his/her support system that can help and encourage. Obtain an agreement with the child to involve them in the process. Communicate the child's need – the target problem – and the plan.

Our role with the significant other in the child's life may be a **consultative role** in which we may advise the teacher on a specific technique to help the child in the classroom, or it may involve providing information to the parents on helpful books or materials.

With significant others in the child's life we may implement the **collaborative role** in which we plan and work together to effect change for the child. Information, ideas, and observations may be shared and a tentative plan of action to support the child implemented.

As counselors, we are to be a child advocate building rapport with the child and significant others in order to create an expectation for positive change as we work together.

When to Refer Out and How

The purpose of school counseling is to assist the student with developmental problems and/or situational problems that with limited sessions can help the child "get back on the right track." As school counselors, we are unable to provide involved counseling or therapy due to our student numbers we serve, our other roles/ responsibilities of school counseling, and in some cases our training. If involved counseling or therapy is needed then the school counselor needs to express this concern with the parent and help the parent connect with an outside agency that can better serve the needs of the child. Be familiar with the services in your community. Most areas have assess to mental health facilities that operate on a sliding fee scale based on what the family can afford as well as private licensed counselors and therapists. If parents request referral names, share three different agencies/therapist names for the parent to pursue. Encourage the parent to talk to the therapist asking questions and getting a feel for the therapist's personality and style. Let the parent know it's okay to ask questions as they gather information to decide what/who is the "right" therapist for their child.

FORMS

STUDENT SELF-REFERRAL FORM

Purpose: These can be copied and cut apart to leave in a pocket folder in each class and/or outside the counseling area so students have a method to contact the counselor. The following pages provide several referral forms for variety and appropriateness for different age levels.

I NEED TO SEE THE COUNSELOR

NAME: ______________________ DATE: __________

TEACHER: ______________________

I need to talk about: ❑ school ❑ home ❑ friends ❑ other

COMMENTS: ______________________

____

____

I NEED TO SEE THE COUNSELOR

NAME: ______________________ DATE: __________

TEACHER: ______________________

I need to talk about: ❑ school ❑ home ❑ friends ❑ other

COMMENTS: ______________________

____

____

STUDENT REQUEST TO SEE THE SCHOOL COUNSELOR

STUDENT: ______________________________ DATE: ____________

HOMEROOM TEACHER: ____________________ GRADE: ________

COMMENTS: ______________________________

____

____

____

❑ CHECK HERE IF YOU FEEL THIS IS AN EMERGENCY AND YOU MUST SEE THE COUNSELOR TODAY.

STUDENT REQUEST TO SEE THE SCHOOL COUNSELOR

STUDENT: ______________________________ DATE: ____________

HOMEROOM TEACHER: ____________________ GRADE: ________

COMMENTS: ______________________________

____

____

____

❑ CHECK HERE IF YOU FEEL THIS IS AN EMERGENCY AND YOU MUST SEE THE COUNSELOR TODAY.

STUDENT REQUEST FOR SCHOOL COUNSELING

Date: ________________

I, ________________________________ *, would like to*
(Name)

see the counselor about ________________________________

____

I am in ________________________ *homeroom class.*
(Teacher's Name)

- ❑ *Emergency: Must see you TODAY!*
- ❑ *Very important: Please see me within a week.*
- ❑ *Important: Please include me in your schedule as soon as you have time.*

STUDENT REQUEST FOR SCHOOL COUNSELING

Date: ________________

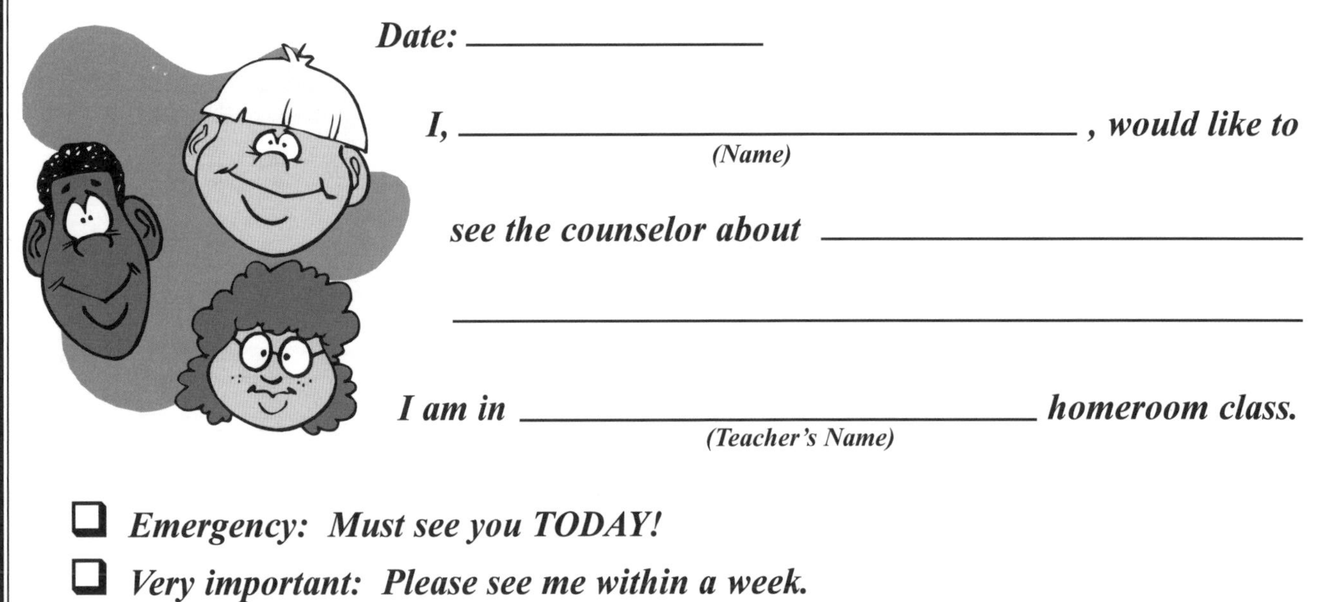

I, ________________________________ *, would like to*
(Name)

see the counselor about ________________________________

____

I am in ________________________ *homeroom class.*
(Teacher's Name)

- ❑ *Emergency: Must see you TODAY!*
- ❑ *Very important: Please see me within a week.*
- ❑ *Important: Please include me in your schedule as soon as you have time.*

I WOULD LIKE TO SEE THE SCHOOL COUNSELOR

I AM FEELING:

☐ MAD

☐ SCARED OR WORRIED

My name is ____

I am in ____________________________________ class.
(Teacher's Name)

I WOULD LIKE TO SEE THE SCHOOL COUNSELOR

I AM FEELING:

☐ SAD

☐ MAD

☐ SCARED OR WORRIED

My name is ____

I am in ____________________________________ class.
(Teacher's Name)

TEACHER REFERRAL

Purpose: The referral form provides communication with the counselor of student concerns. Keep in mind there are many other ways staff refer students – by email, phone, in the hall, etc. As counselors we work to respond to the needs of students.

Teacher Referral Form
for School Counseling

Student's Name: ______________________________ *Date:* ______________

Referring Teacher: ______________________________

Student's Homeroom Teacher: ______________________ *Grade:* ____________

1. *Reason for referral:* ______________________________

____

____

2. *Action taken by the teacher (disciplinary, parent conference, etc.):* ____________

____

____

3. *Student's attitude toward the problem:* ______________________________

____

4. *One thing the student does especially well:* ______________________________

____

Urgent? *Yes* *No*

Student knowledge of referral:
- ☐ *Has not been discussed with the student*
- ☐ *Student is aware of the referral*

TEACHER REFERRAL FORM for COUNSELING SERVICES

Student's Name: ______________________________ **Date:** __________

Referring Teacher: ______________________________

Reason(s) for referral:

- ☐ Disruptive classroom behavior
- ☐ Difficulty in getting along with other students
- ☐ Consistent neglect of schoolwork
- ☐ Extreme dislike or fear of school
- ☐ Inattentive; excessive daydreaming
- ☐ Anti-social behavior
- ☐ Lack of motivation in school
- ☐ Personal or home problems
- ☐ Other:

Comments:

Action(s) taken by the Teacher: ______________________________

____

Student's attitude toward the problem: ______________________________

____

I would like:

- ☐ you to observe this student.
- ☐ to discuss this student with you. I am available at ________
- ☐ you to participate in a parent conference on ________
- ☐ you to talk with this student.

Student knowledge of referral:

- ☐ has not been discussed with the student
- ☐ student is aware of the referral
- ☐ parent is aware of the referral

Please fold this confidential form and return to the counseling office.

PARENT REFERRAL for SCHOOL COUNSELING

Purpose: The form provides a method to document parent concerns regarding their child. Parent contact may occur by phone, conference, or parent teacher conference. Remember it is important for the home and school to work together for the child. You may need to clarify for the parent that school counseling helps address concerns that may be interfering with the learning and that school counseling can assist students in developmental and situational type problems. School counseling does not provide involved therapy. Outside referrals need to be considered if therapy is needed.

PARENT REFERRAL for SCHOOL COUNSELING

Student Name ______________________________ Date ______________

Parent's Name ______________________________ Homeroom ______________

Phone Number (h) ____________________ (w) ____________________

Referral made by: ☐ phone contact

☐ conference

Description of the concern: ______________________________

____

____

Interventions parent has tried: ______________________________

____

____

Future Interventions/plan discussed: ______________________________

____

____

Other Info:

Form:

FEEDBACK from COUNSELING REFERRAL

Purpose: Sent to teacher who referred the student. The form provides a brief feedback to update the person who made the initial referral. Adults working together for the child is the most productive.

FEEDBACK FROM COUNSELING REFERRAL

To: ____

From: ____

Re: ____
(Student Name)

- ❑ ***Student appears to have resolved/managed the problem. Please let me know if there are further concerns.***
- ❑ ***Student will be seen on a regular basis for individual counseling.***
- ❑ ***Parents were contacted regarding referral.***
- ❑ ***Student would benefit from small group counseling.***
- ❑ ***Student has been referred to another professional.***
- ❑ ***Other:*** ________________________________

Comments:

If you have questions or would like to discuss this student further, please let me know.

APPOINTMENT NOTICE

Purpose: Given to the student or placed in the teacher's box for the student to tell / remind him / her of the time for the individual counseling appointment.

SCHOOL COUNSELING APPOINTMENT

Teacher: ____________________

____
(Student's Name)

has an appointment with the school counselor at the following time:

Date ____________________

Time ____________________

☐ Please send the student.

☐ I will come to the room to get the student.

SCHOOL COUNSELING APPOINTMENT

Teacher: ____________________

____
(Student's Name)

has an appointment with the school counselor at the following time:

Date ____________________

Time ____________________

☐ Please send the student.

☐ I will come to the room to get the student.

SCHOOL COUNSELING APPOINTMENT

Teacher: ____________________

____
(Student's Name)

has an appointment with the school counselor at the following time:

Date ____________________

Time ____________________

☐ Please send the student.

☐ I will come to the room to get the student.

SCHOOL COUNSELING APPOINTMENT

Teacher: ____________________

____
(Student's Name)

has an appointment with the school counselor at the following time:

Date ____________________

Time ____________________

☐ Please send the student.

☐ I will come to the room to get the student.

SCHOOL COUNSELING APPOINTMENT

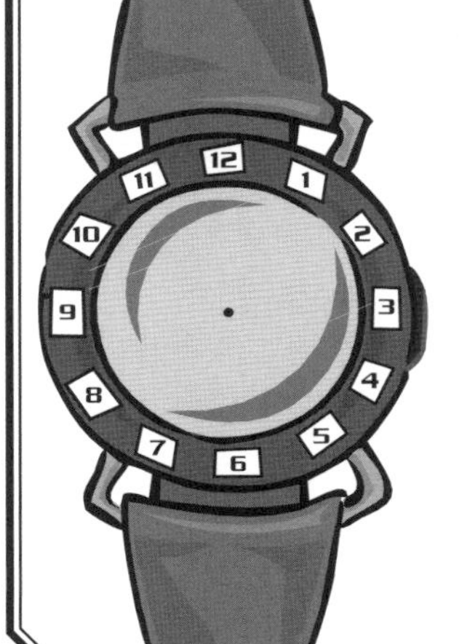

The time for

____
(Student's Name)

appointment with the school counselor is:

Date ______________________________

Time ______________________________

SCHOOL COUNSELING APPOINTMENT

The time for

____
(Student's Name)

appointment with the school counselor is:

Date ______________________________

Time ______________________________

SCHOOL COUNSELING APPOINTMENT

The time for

____
(Student's Name)

appointment with the school counselor is:

Date ______________________________

Time ______________________________

SCHOOL COUNSELING APPOINTMENT

The time for

____
(Student's Name)

appointment with the school counselor is:

Date ______________________________

Time ______________________________

INDIVIDUAL COUNSELING PLAN / NOTES

Purpose: The form allows for note-taking of contacts regarding the student, provides for individual counseling session or contact summaries, and a plan for future work with the student. The "type of contact" can be marked as: individual counseling, parent consultation, teacher consultation, conference, etc. depending on the type of contact. The first "summary" entry allows additional space to document the concern and information gathered. The "plan" allows you to mark the direction or emphasis you feel is the next step for the student. It may include contact with the teacher or parent, or may involve an area to explore with the child, or a specific activity that may be helpful in working with the student. Note-taking and creating tentative plans can help us maintain our focus and direction in counseling.

Tips for Note Taking:

Document significant information using quotes such as: "the student shared, '…'. If significant information is in the form of your observation due to the affect or tone in their voice then state it in the notes as: "Counselor observed …" stating the facial expression or behavior. Avoid adding opinion to the documentation. Our notes are intended for our private use and are not a part of the school records however use your professionalism in note taking. In unusual circumstances, the notes could be seen by others. The purpose of the notes is to help us as counselors target the problem and to develop a plan of action to assist. Our professional skills are constantly needed as well as our flexibility to change the plan/strategy as needs change and/or are better understood.

INDIVIDUAL COUNSELING PLAN / NOTES

STUDENT'S NAME ______________________________

GRADE / HOMEROOM ______________________________

PARENT(S) ______________________ Resides With ____________

TELEPHONE: Home ____________ M's Work ____________ F's Work ____________

DATE:

TYPE OF CONTACT:

SUMMARY:

PLAN:

DATE:

TYPE OF CONTACT:

SUMMARY:

PLAN:

DATE:

TYPE OF CONTACT:

SUMMARY:

PLAN:

DATE:
TYPE OF CONTACT:

SUMMARY:

PLAN:

DATE:
TYPE OF CONTACT:

SUMMARY:

PLAN:

DATE:
TYPE OF CONTACT:

SUMMARY:

PLAN:

DATE:
TYPE OF CONTACT:

SUMMARY:

PLAN:

Information Gathering

This section provides a variety of strategies, questions, activities, and techniques to connect with the child, build rapport, and gain insight into the child's perception of his / her world. Keep in mind that it is the child's perception of what's wrong that we need to deal with, not our own external interpretation of what's wrong. The activities, in the first part of this section, promote an opportunity for interaction in which to gain this insight.

This section also includes formal and informal inventories that can provide a systematic way to gather information. Keep in mind that the process of gathering information is just as important as the collected information. Through the process you can observe affect and ask questions to clarify their reason behind the rating thus gaining more information. Through this process the student and the counselor may obtain a more accurate picture of the strengths and weaknesses and set target goals for future counseling sessions. Inventories are also included for teachers and parents to complete which give additional perspectives regarding the strengths and weaknesses of the student. This allows you to compare information, to confront the child of other's perceptions about him/her, and/or to challenge a misperception of the child's.

A vital source of information can be gained from significant adults in the child's life. A guideline of possible questions are given in this section to use when consulting with parents and teachers. Not only does consulting help gain additional information to understand the problem but it also can establish a collaborative relationship and commitment to work together for the student.

Activity:

ASSESSING THE CHILD*

Purpose: To review basic areas in which you need to assess and gather information about the student and his/her world in order to best help the student with his / her problem

Procedure: You may choose to formally use this as a form documenting information or simply review the needed areas to assess and collect the information in your head as you begin to understand the child and his / her world.

PHYSICAL: Review the student's physical appearance and how he/she presents him/her self. Ask yourself such questions as: What type of posture? What is the affect/facial expressions? What is the energy level?

____

____

____

SOCIAL: Assess the student's ability to connect easily with others. Ask yourself such questions as: What is the level of communication of the student? Is his/her manner generally positive or negative? Does the individual have any friends or fit into groups around the school?

____

____

____

COGNITIVE: Assess the cognitive level of the child. Ask yourself such questions as: Where is the child developmentally with their thinking – concrete? abstract? Can the child understand behavior and consequences? Does he/she typically use rational or irrational thinking?

____

____

____

CULTURAL: Assess the child's culture and how it may impact the counseling process. Ask yourself such questions as: What religious, cultural, or environmental factors have influenced the person's thinking, feeling, and behaving? What cultural information do I need to be aware of in dealing with this child that may effect his/her affect, verbal responses, family support, etc.?

HISTORY: Assess if any general or specific history of the child's is relevant to the present situation or problem. Ask yourself: Have there been any particular events that may have contributed to the problem or difficulties such as family changes, death, traumatic events, etc.?

FUTURE PERSPECTIVE: Assess the child's viewpoint of his/her future. Ask yourself such questions as: Is the child more optimistic or pessimistic? Does the child see the problem as solvable? Is he/she willing to take control and responsibility for his/her future?

THE PRESENTING PROBLEM: Assess the child's ability to pinpoint the problem. Ask yourself: Does the child know what has led them to counseling? Is he/she able to verbalize the problem?

---

*adapted from Robert Myrick (2003). *Developmental Guidance and Counseling: A Practical Approach*, Fourth Edition. Minneapolis, MN: Educational Media Corporation, pp. 174-175.

Activity: FAMILY FIGURES

Purpose: Exploring self and family, gathering insight and information

Materials: Paper and pencil / crayons / markers

Procedure: Ask the child to draw a picture of him / herself or you can draw a stick figure picture on the paper representing the child. If you are drawing the child, ask what type of feeling face to add to the picture. Continue drawing and ask the following questions:

- **Who in your family do we need to draw next?**
  - If you are drawing the stick figure family ask:
    - **Where should I draw them?**
    - **What kind of feeling face do they have?**

      Add and label each picture.
- **Tell me about the person.**
- **What kinds of things do you do together?**
- **What's your favorite thing about the person?**
- **What's your not-so-favorite thing about the person?**

If the child is from a split family from parent's separation, divorce, etc. then draw the other household on the back of the paper.

Summarize the family information from the picture drawings. If any significant information surfaced, share a tentative observation such as: "Sounds like you get really scared when your older brother picks on you. Would it help to talk about that more and how to deal with that?" This provides opportunity for the counselor and student to work together to determine needs and set goals and objectives for the sessions.

Activity: PICTURE OF ME

Purpose: Using drawing to explore about him / herself

Materials: Paper and pencil, crayons, markers

Procedure: Ask the student to draw a picture of him/herself on the paper. Explore, choosing from the following questions:

- What kind of feeling face did you draw?
- What are you thinking about in that picture?
- What kinds of things do you enjoy doing?
- What kinds of things do you not like to do?
- Pretend this is a picture of you in the classroom at school.
  - Who is sitting next to you?
  - Where is the teacher?
  - What's going on in the picture?
  - What is your favorite thing about school?
  - Your not-so-favorite thing about school?
- Pretend this is a picture of you at recess.
  - What is going on in the picture?
- Pretend this is a picture of you at the bus stop.
  - What is going on in the picture?
- Pretend this is a picture of you riding the bus.
  - What's happening in the picture?
- Pretend this is a picture of you at home.
  - What are you doing?
  - What is your favorite thing about home?
  - Your not-so-favorite thing about home?
- Pretend this is a picture of you with a friend.
  - Tell me about it.

If significant information is shared in this process, continue exploring with questions such as:

- If the student has described a perfect picture ask, "Is this how it is or how you wish it could be? Do you want to work on how to make the wish a reality?"
- If the picture described presents a problem area then explore more by reflecting the feelings behind the situation and ask, "Is this something you want to work on together?"

Activity: WINDOWS TO OUR WORLD

Purpose: Drawing activity to share about HOME, SCHOOL, SELF, FRIENDS

Materials: Wall display with four sheets of removable paper depicting panes of a window. Clothespins attached to the wall work well to hold the removable paper. Label the four sheets HOME, SCHOOL, SELF, FRIENDS. You may choose to add a window curtain on the wall for effect.

Procedure: Guide the student to look at the window wall display and ask:

- **What is the purpose of windows in a home?**

Explore that in a home you can look outside and also people can look inside from the outside. Talk about how when you walk / or ride by a home with an open window curtain you may see in their window to a family sitting around a table eating or watching TV, etc.

Relate a window in a home to the window on the wall by saying:

- **This window is not a window to our home but a window to our world. This is a chance to look inside our world at HOME, at SCHOOL, with FRIENDS, and to open up about OURSELVES. You may choose any of the four window panes, we can take it down, and you can draw a picture about that window pane (HOME, SCHOOL, SELF, FRIENDS) to share something about yourself and your world.**

This activity can provide insight to help determine needs, goals and objectives.

Activity: PUPPET POWER

Purpose: Puppets provide a third party way to communicate, thus relieving the stress or tension sometimes created by the single focus on the child

Materials: A collection of puppets with movable mouths. May also include a selection of a variety of animal puppets such as a lion, a mouse, a dog, a wolf, a lamb

Procedure: If the student is exploring your room and he / she picks up a puppet from your puppet display, use this opportunity to get to know more about the student by dialoguing with the puppet. The following gives some suggested statements / questions:

Speaking to the puppet,

"Hi there Mr. / Mrs. Puppet. I didn't know you knew _______ (name of child). Can you tell me about _______ and what they like? Who all is in his / her family? Tell me about what it is like at home? Does he/she like to be at school or not? What's his/her favorite thing about school? What is his / her not-so-favorite thing about school?"

Another way to use puppets is...

Guide the child over to the puppet section and ask them to choose an animal puppet most like him / her. Dialogue with the puppet some and then ask the puppet if he knows why _____ (child's name) chose you as the animal puppet most like him / her. Encourage him / her to tell you. If the puppet says that he doesn't know then you can turn to the child and ask the child to tell the puppet why he / she chose him. You can also gain additional information by asking questions about what you know of that animal and if it is true of the child. Use this opportunity to point out the strengths of the animal. For example, if they choose the mouse you can say,

"I've heard the saying 'as quiet as a mouse' for I know that the mouse can be very quiet and they have their eyes open being very sharp to see everything around them and they have expert ears to focus on listening well. Are you quiet, do you have sharp eyes, and listen well?"

TELEPHONE

Purpose: To provide a non-threatening method of communication

Materials: 2 play telephones

Procedure: This strategy can be successful with the younger student. As you are allowing the student to look at the toys in the play area make the sound of a telephone ringing as you hold one receiver to your ear and walk away to provide a little distance. Point out where the other phone is if they have not already discovered it. When they answer the phone, begin a conversation introducing yourself and then asking the child to tell about him/herself or his/her day, etc. Ask questions to get to know the student and to gather additional information.

Activity: POPSICLE SENTENCES

Purpose: To provide a creative method of using incomplete sentences to gain information

Materials: Popsicle sticks in a can with an incomplete sentence written on each stick

Procedure: Ask the student to draw a stick, then read (or you read for the student) and complete the sentence. This is simply a sentence completion activity but the use of the child drawing the sticks to read the sentence adds a game-like playful tone to the activity that can encourage communication.

Sentences for the sticks:

1. I like friends who _____.
2. One thing you should know about me is _____.
3. It bothers me when _____.
4. Tests make me feel _____.
5. I get into trouble when I _____.
6. I don't like to _____.
7. When someone makes fun of me I _____.
8. When I am mad I _____.
9. I don't enjoy school when _____.
10. If I could have one wish, it would be _____.
11. I am very good at _____.
12. One thing you should know about me is _____.
13. I felt proud when _____.
14. Happiness is _____.
15. Something that really makes me feel bad is _____.
16. Something that really makes me feel good is _____.
17. I get angry when _____.
18. I get mad at myself when _____.
19. I get scared when _____.
20. I get sad when _____.
21. I really get upset when _____.
22. My mother always _____.
23. My dad always _____.
24. My teacher always _____.
25. It is hard for me to _____.
26. One thing I worry about is _____.
27. One way I get attention is to _____.
28. I like teachers who _____.

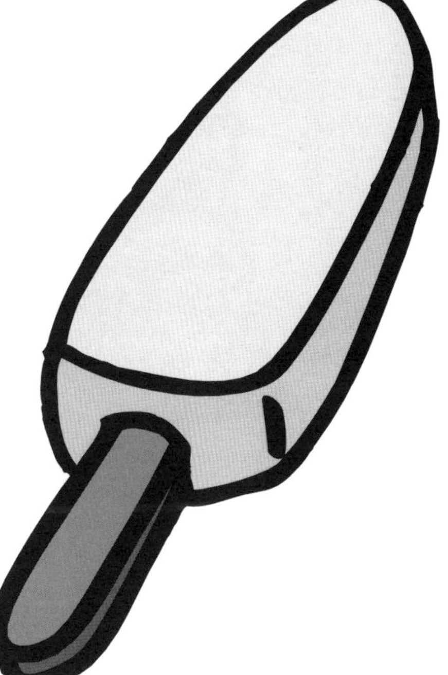

Activity: GETTING TO KNOW ME

Purpose: To gather information through a Getting To Know Me Worksheet

Materials: Copy of the Getting To Know Me Worksheet

Procedure: This worksheet can be completed together or by the individual. Allow time for discussion and sharing.

GETTING TO KNOW ME

Name: ______________________________ Date: ______________

The people in my family are:

One thing I like about myself is:

One thing I want to change about myself is:

The things I like best at school are:

In school, I wish I could change:

The things I like best at home are:

At home, I wish I could change:

About my friends, I want to tell you:

Activity: PICTURES... PICTURES

Purpose: Pictures provide a tool for discussion to understand the child and his / her perception of his / her world.

Materials: Copy of the following pictures and / or pictures from a magazine of children in different places that can be used in individual counseling

Procedure: Clip pictures from magazines that you think could be used in a counseling session. Several pictures are given here with possible questions to get you started:

Picture 1: Classroom

"What's going on in this classroom?"
"Which student do you think is most like you?"

Picture 2: Recess

"What's happening in this picture?"
"Where would you add yourself in this picture?"

Picture 3: Home

"I need your help to draw your family in this picture."
"Tell me about your picture."

Activity:

PERCEPTOGRAPH -STUDENT INVENTORY

Purpose: To gain insight and information into the child's perception of SELF, OTHERS, and SCHOOL

Materials: Copy of the Student Inventory Worksheet

Procedure: The student inventory can be given to the child to complete on his/her own but I prefer reading the statements to the child and having the student respond. Encourage them to respond honestly. You can select only a few questions from each section or use it in its entirety.

After the inventory has been completed, review first by pointing out what you see through their answers as their strengths. Next begin reviewing the other scores that were marked lower. Ask the student:

- **What were you thinking when you marked it a _______________?**

Remain non-judgmental, asking questions for clarification and more information.

Students are welcome to change their answers if they misunderstood the question or have changed their perception. Again review their strengths, then ask the student to look at the ones marked lower choosing first, second, and third choice of what they may want to work on in the counseling session.

Also included is a TEACHER / PARENT INVENTORY that can be used to compare information, to confront the child of others perceptions about him / her, and / or to challenge a misperception of the child's. If you use this inventory formally with the child and include teachers and parents you may want to get parent's permission. Check with your school / district's policy.

Rating:

The actual rating can be completed in several ways:

- **4 -1, as shown on the worksheet, can be used for the older child who has a cognitive ability to understand and apply the four different rating degrees.**

- **3 -1 rating scale can be used for the younger child.**
  3 = "Great"
  2 = "Okay"
  1 = "Poor"

- **A thumbs-up and thumbs-down rating scale can be used for the youngest students for them to communicate their thoughts.**

STUDENT INVENTORY

Name: ______________________________ **Date:** ______________

Directions: Complete the following questions by circling the answer that you feel correctly describes your thoughts, feelings, or behavior.

	Strongly Agree	Agree	Disagree	Strongly Disagree
WHAT I THINK ABOUT ME				
I like who I am.	4	3	2	1
I am an important and special person.	4	3	2	1
I can handle it well when I make a mistake.	4	3	2	1
I have the courage to try new things.	4	3	2	1
I can handle it well if I get criticized or teased by others.	4	3	2	1
I can handle it even if things are difficult or hard.	4	3	2	1
I manage both my pleasant & unpleasant feelings well.	4	3	2	1
WHAT I THINK ABOUT ME and OTHERS				
I get along well with others.	4	3	2	1
Others are interested in what I have to say.	4	3	2	1
I know how to make and keep friends.	4	3	2	1
I am a good friend to others.	4	3	2	1
I handle friendship problems well.	4	3	2	1
I get along well with mom.	4	3	2	1
I get along well with dad.	4	3	2	1
I get along well with my brothers / sisters.	4	3	2	1
WHAT I THINK ABOUT ME and SCHOOL				
I start my school work as soon as assigned.	4	3	2	1
I work hard and finish my school assignments.	4	3	2	1
I complete my homework.	4	3	2	1
I have my materials needed to do my work.	4	3	2	1
I participate in class discussions.	4	3	2	1
I behave in class - following the rules.	4	3	2	1
I stay focused and listen carefully in class.	4	3	2	1
I like school.	4	3	2	1
I like my teachers.	4	3	2	1
My teachers like me.	4	3	2	1
School is a friendly place to be.	4	3	2	1

PERCEPTOGRAPH -PARENT/TEACHER INVENTORY

Information Gathering

Purpose: To gain insight from significant adults in the child's life of their perception of the child

Materials: Copy of the Parent / Teacher Inventory Worksheet

Procedure: Send the letter and inventory to the parent/teacher requesting the parent / teacher to rate the child in the areas specified. Either add the person's name of who you are sending the letter / inventory to or circle "Parent / Teacher" in the letter / inventory to indicate who the letter / inventory is for / from.

Dear Parent / Teacher,

In working with ________________________________ in individual counseling it is helpful to gather information from important people in the child's life. It is helpful to understand your perception of how the child feels and thinks about him / herself, your perception about how he / she relates to others, and about how you think he/she is doing at school. Thank you for taking the time to complete this inventory. Information will be used to better understand the child as we work together to help the child be successful. Please mark below how you agree that this information should be used.

______ You have my permission to share my ratings with others involved - the child, the teacher / parent. At times it is helpful to show the child that other important people in his / her life see that he / she is friendly or has good behavior, etc. or at times it helps to confront the child with other people's perception that he / she does not complete the class work or follow the rules, etc.

______ I would rather you not share this information with others but use it for your own understanding of the child.

________________________________ ________________________

Signature *Date*

If you have questions or would like to discuss further, feel free to call.

Sincerely,

Your School Counselor

PARENT / TEACHER INVENTORY for

Student's Name: ________________________________ **Date:** ______________

Directions: Complete the following questions by circling the answer that you feel correctly describes the child's thoughts, feelings, or behavior.

	Strongly Agree	Agree	Disagree	Strongly Disagree
WHAT CHILD THINKS ABOUT HIM/HER SELF				
He/she likes who he/she is.	4	3	2	1
He/she is an important and special person.	4	3	2	1
He/she can handle it well when he/she makes a mistake.	4	3	2	1
He/she has the courage to try new things.	4	3	2	1
He/she can handle it well if he/she gets criticized or teased.	4	3	2	1
He/she can handle it even if things are difficult or hard.	4	3	2	1
He/she manages both pleasant & unpleasant feelings well.	4	3	2	1
WHAT CHILD THINKS ABOUT SELF and OTHERS				
He/she gets along well with others.	4	3	2	1
Others are interested in what he/she has to say.	4	3	2	1
He/she knows how to make and keep friends.	4	3	2	1
He/she is a good friend to others.	4	3	2	1
He/she handles friendship problems well.	4	3	2	1
He/she gets along well with mom.	4	3	2	1
He/she gets along well with dad.	4	3	2	1
He/she gets along well with his/her brothers/sisters.	4	3	2	1
WHAT CHILD THINKS ABOUT SCHOOL				
He/she starts school work as soon as assigned.	4	3	2	1
He/she works hard and finishes school assignments.	4	3	2	1
He/she completes homework.	4	3	2	1
He/she has materials needed to do his/her work.	4	3	2	1
He/she participates in class discussions.	4	3	2	1
He/she behaves in class - following the rules.	4	3	2	1
He/she stays focused and listens carefully in class.	4	3	2	1
He/she likes school.	4	3	2	1
He/she likes his/her teachers.	4	3	2	1
He/she feels the teachers like him/her.	4	3	2	1
He/she feels school is a friendly place.	4	3	2	1

Activity:

CONSULTING WITH TEACHERS and PARENTS

Information Gathering

Purpose: To gain insight from significant others in the child's life and to establish a collaborative relationship to work together for the benefit of the child

Procedure: Below list types of questions that could be asked to help gather information and to understand the problem. Counseling skills are important to use in this process as you not only gain information of the problem and what may work and not work in managing the problem but you also gain insight into the adult's perception of the child and the problem. The child's support system is very important in the child's life and needs to be directed in a solution-focused path. The list does not include all the questions that could or should be asked but only gives samples of the types of questions that can be asked. In consulting with the teacher / parent in gathering information, a collaborative relationship may be beneficial as you choose to work together for the benefit of the child.

Possible Questions:

1. What do you see as the needs of the child?
2. What are his/her strengths? Weaknesses?
3. Is this a new behavior or concern or something that you have been dealing with over an extended period?
4. Is there a time when the behavior/problem seems better or worse?
5. Can you pinpoint any triggers for the behavior/problem?
6. What have you found works for you and is effective in helping the child?
7. Describe a time when the child may have successfully managed the problem. What skills did the child use? Who may have helped? How can we build on this?
8. What are some ways to specifically deal with the problem when it arises?
9. What are some ways to restructure the environment providing a positive atmosphere?
10. Who are people in the child's life that he/she can count on for support?

ACTIVITIES FOR UNDERSTANDING AND DEALING WITH THE PROBLEM

This section begins with the activity, "Problem Solving Questions" that includes six steps to "problem solving." This model is effective typically for students who already know their "problem" and are ready to come up with a plan, however the majority of our counseling typically doesn't work that way. The other activities in this section provide creative activities and approaches to help explore what the problem might be, to explore their perception of the problem, their attitude, and to explore with them effective ways to cope with or deal with the problem. The following only provides the basic activities, it is your insight and counseling skills that are needed. As the counselor, you can use your skills to "hear the words beneath the words." You can observe the affect to help guide the child in understanding and movement towards resolution and positive mental health. In the counseling session, as insights are gained as to the problem, you can begin setting informal goals and objectives. Keep in mind that these plans need to be fluid, and we must be ready to change the goals and objectives depending on changes and new insights.

As you begin the counseling process, you may choose to utilize the "Individual Counseling Plan/Notes" form that is located in the FORMS section of this book. This form allows you to document contacts, summarize counseling information, and formulate plans for future counseling sessions.

Activity: PROBLEM-SOLVING QUESTIONS

Purpose: To provide an outline of questions to use in the problem-solving process

Procedure: If you are in a school setting and the student has made a self-referral then he / she is entering the counseling session with a specific problem to discuss. The following guideline of questions can be effective in working through the problem-solving process. Keep in mind that there are times that students may refer themselves with a presenting problem but they may be "testing" you to see if there is a good relationship, comfort level, and trustworthiness in order to share the "real concern or problem." Use of good counseling skills – reflective listening, observing affect, open-ended questions, summarizing, clarifying, etc. - in this process is essential. The following questions can be used as guidelines in the counseling process to explore the problem and create a plan:

What is the problem?

What have you tried?

What else could you do?

Brainstorm possible ways to handle the problem. Ask the student to share first. Listen and guide the student to create a list of socially acceptable possibilities. If they need assistance in developing a list always begin tentatively with your suggestions such as, Would this be a possibility to....? or Other students have shared... what do you think?

What would happen if you tried that?

Review the possibilities that were brainstormed in the above step and explore the positive and negative consequences of each.

From the possibilities that have been discussed, what do you want to try first?

As the student chooses from the above possibilities remind him/her of the positive and negative consequences. Ask if they are prepared to handle the negative consequence, if that occurs. It is important to allow thestudent to choose which strategy to try. Even though the student may have shared the problem he/she may not have disclosed everything. The student is "in" his / her life and knows best about the interactions with significant others. Our job is to help the student explore the possibilities and to guide and support him/her as the student thinks through the problem and solutions.

What is your plan?

Assist the student to determine when, where, and how to implement the chosen problem solving strategy. Practicing and role-playing implementing the strategy may be appropriate to prepare the student. Schedule a follow-up with the student to assess if Plan A was successful; if not review the above steps and create a Plan B.

Activity: FEELINGS PROVIDE INSIGHT

Purpose: To gain insight into the child's feelings, thoughts, and perception

Materials: Pictures of feeling faces

Procedure: Focus on different feeling faces such as happy, sad, angry, afraid, worried. As you focus on one face at a time ask the following questions for each of the feelings:

What is the feeling?

Tell me a time when someone might feel that way.

Reflectively listen, asking questions and exploring.

When else might someone feel that way?

Continue asking for examples until the student appears to have exhausted possibilities.

Summarize the different feelings and examples shared. If any significant information surfaced, share a tentative observation such as:

> "Getting angry seems to be something that really bugs you, is this something you might want to talk more about and figure out ways to handle?"

This provides opportunity for the counselor and student to work together to determine needs and set goals and objectives for the sessions.

Commercially purchased feeling faces can be used such as Felicia the Feeling Flower from Marco, or the Bear Feelings from Childswork Childsplay. Or you can use pictures of feeling faces on pages 68 and 69 in the Feelings Section of this book.

CLAY CHAT

Purpose: Using clay as a means to relax and to communicate

Materials: Clay, Play-Doh™, or Model Magic™, cookie cutter shapes (ie. boy, girl, heart, flower, airplane, etc.)

Procedure: Any type of clay helps communication by providing a fun, relaxed, playful atmosphere. As counselor and child are playing with clay or Play-Doh™ it can ease the talking relationship. If the conversation lends itself to discussing a problem area then you can use the clay and cookie cutters to cut the different shapes to use with your counseling skills. For example:

The boy or girl shapes can be used to reenact the child's problem and then role-play possible solutions.

The airplane can be used to ask the child to fly over the town, neighborhood, home, or school and ask to share what we would see.

The heart shape can be used by creating a tear in the clay heart to symbolize the hurt we feel from the problem. Next discuss ways to repair the hurt or cope with the problem – while this discussion is happening, begin to mend the clay heart (the heart is a good symbol for the pain in parent's divorce).

The petals of the flower can be used to list the good qualities or talents of the child's. Relate the flower to the child's blooming and sharing his / her beauty.

Activity:

COUNSELING LEADS

Purpose: The following provide various statements/questions to facilitate the counseling process.

1. What would you like to talk about today?
2. How does it look to you?
3. What do you think you would like to do about it?
4. What are some other possibilities?
5. Tell me more about it.
6. Tell me about yourself.
7. Tell me about your family.
8. How does this affect you?
9. What if that doesn't work, what else can you try?
10. How does this fit in with your future?
11. How would you summarize our discussion?
12. If you could do this over again what would you do differently?
13. If the same thing came up again, what would you do?
14. How do you fit into this picture?
15. In what ways do you think you could improve the situation?
16. What are your next steps?
17. How do you explain those feelings to yourself?
18. Think of a time when you handled the situation well. What did you do?
19. We seem to be getting away from the reason for our time together. I wonder if you could tell me more about...
20. Tell me about what you like to do for fun – things that you enjoy doing in your free time.
21. When you think the child is falsifying a story you can gently confront with ...I am really having trouble with this because I have never heard of anything like it before. OR I am really having trouble with this because it is hard for me to imagine that person doing this.

Activity: THINGS THAT BUG ME*

Purpose: To allow the student to specify things that bother him / her

Materials: Copy, laminate, cut out bugs on pages 49-50, and place in a jar. If possible, use plastic bugs with the information taped onto the different bugs.

Procedure: Relate being bugged by bugs while on a picnic or playing outside to being bugged or bothered by things that happen in our life. Have the student pick a bug from the jar and respond to the statement. Encourage a response and sharing about each statement by asking such questions as:

- What do you think that means?

- What would a person be thinking, doing, or saying if that "bugged" them?

- Have you ever seen anyone who you think was being "bugged" by that?

- What did you see or hear that made you think that was bugging them?

- How about you – is this something that has "bugged" you before?

Use of your counseling skills is essential to observe affect, listen to the words, and to ask questions for more information. Continue the activity by having the student prioritize the things that "bugs" him / her the most and the least. Allow the student to complete the "bug" of "I get bugged when... in order to gain additional insight into the problem.

*adapted with permission from Senn (2003). *Small Group Counseling for Children, Grades 2-5*. Chapin, SC: YouthLight, Inc. www.youthlightbooks.com

Handout:
THINGS THAT BUG ME

I get "bugged" when I'm left out.

I get "bugged" when my parents and teachers correct my behavior.

I get "bugged" when I don't get my way.

I get "bugged" when I feel things are unfair.

I get "bugged" when I get in trouble for doing something wrong.

I get "bugged" when people tease me.

Handout: THINGS THAT BUG ME

Activity: THINK OUTSIDE OF THE BOX*

Purpose: To encourage the child to use creative thinking in problem solving

Materials: String or cord (shoe string works nicely)

Procedure: Ask the student to tie a knot in the string. Most students can do this with ease. Relate that some of our problems can be simple to handle. However, some of our problems are more difficult, therefore put the stipulation on the string that they must continue to hold each end of the string in each hand while they try to tie the knot. Most people attempt to move their hands in and out trying but if they maintain holding each end they will not be successful this way.

Ask the student if they would like some help. Share with the student that it's okay to ask for help when it's difficult just as it's okay to ask for help with difficult problems. Add that at times we have to be creative and try something different to deal with our problems.

Ask the student to cross their arms. Hand them the ends of the string in each hand and ask them to unfold their arms, this will result in the knot being tied in the string. Relate the success with the knot to success with problems. When you are creative, ask for help, and perhaps try something different, success is increased.

Next discuss creative strategies for managing the presenting problem.

*adapted with permission from Robert P. Bowman, Ph.D. (2005). *201 Amazing Mind Bogglers*, The Fast Knot: Mind Boggler #47. Chapin, SC: YouthLight, Inc. www.youthlightbooks.com.

Activity: ROCK OR CLAY PROBLEM*

Purpose: To help the student distinguish between problems that they can change or control and problems in which they must learn to cope

Materials: Piece of clay and a rock

Procedure: Give the student a piece of clay and explain that it represents a problem. Ask the student to make something out of the clay. Then discuss, asking:

- *How did you come up with what to make?*

- *Did the clay tell you what to make?*

Come to the conclusion that the student CONTROLLED the clay. Give examples of some problems that we can control such as not doing our homework, talking in class, etc.

Next, ask the student to make something different with the clay. Discuss what the student just did – they CHANGED the clay. Give examples of things that can be changed sometimes to fix a problem such as: if you can't see well you get glasses, if you don't like the way your handwriting is, you change it.

Change up the student's clay for a rock. Ask the student to make something out of the rock like he/she did with the clay. Students usually struggle some and/or look at you funny and say they can't. At this point explain that some problems are clay problems that can be controlled by making a change. But some problems are rock problems that cannot be controlled or changed and that we have to learn to COPE with these problems. Some examples of rock problems are: parents getting a divorce or someone not wanting to be your friend. Share that with these problems we need to focus on coping with the problem and finding ways to be okay with the problem.

Point out that when we first realize we have a problem it may be helpful to determine if it is a clay or a rock problem. If it is a rock problem then we don't need to use our energy and time on trying to control or change something that we can't, instead we need to focus on accepting the problem and learning how to manage or cope with the problem. If it is a clay problem then we need to create a plan for change.

*adapted with permission from Sitsch and Senn (2002). *Puzzle Pieces: The Classroom Guidance Connection.* Chapin, SC: YouthLight, Inc. www.youthlightbooks.com

Activity: SHRINKING THE PROBLEM

Purpose: To "shrink" the problem so that it becomes manageable

Materials: Paper, pencil, crayons

Procedure: Ask the student to draw a picture of the problem on a full sheet of paper. Encourage the student to talk about the problem by asking him / her to describe the picture asking about the thoughts and feelings that may be going on in the problem. Next have the student fold the picture in half and again in half. While the picture is being folded, brainstorm ways to deal with the problem thus reducing stress and managing the problem effectively. Finally ask the student to redraw the problem on the quarter sheet of folded paper. Compare the large problem to the smaller problem, processing the different thoughts and feelings. Encourage the student to write next to the smaller picture of the problem helpful ways to "shrink" the problem.

PROBLEM-SOLVING WITH PERSONAL STRENGTHS*

Purpose: To connect the use of personal strengths to managing problems

Materials: Paper and pencil

Procedure: Ask the student to fold a sheet of paper in half long ways (hotdog style). On half of the sheet of paper ask the student to list the problems that he / she is dealing with. Then have the student turn the paper over to the second folded side and ask them to list their strengths – positive words that describe them (encourage them to write at least five words).

Personal strength words may include but are not limited to:

- **caring**
- **responsible**
- **artistic**
- **open-minded**
- **honest**
- **self-disciplined**
- **creative**
- **shares**
- **helpful**
- **brave**
- **energetic**
- **thoughtful**
- **respectful**
- **kind**
- **friendly**
- **unselfish**
- **polite**
- **accepting of others**
- **giving**
- **witty**

Next ask the student to open the sheet which should appear with the problems listed on the left and the child's strengths listed on the right. Ask the student to review his/her strengths determining which strengths could help in dealing with each problem. Ask the student to draw a line from the strength to the problems and encourage them to explain how they will be using that strength to manage the problem.

*adapted with permission from the Strength Coaching Model as presented in *Individual Counseling Activities for Children*, by Bowman and Bowman, available through www.youthlightbooks.com.

PERSPECTIVES IN PROBLEM-SOLVING

Purpose: This activity is for problems that involve others and is intended to encourage the child to view different perspectives regarding the problem

Materials: Need to copy on card stock or construction paper 2 sets of shoe prints on the next page.

Procedure: Place the 2 sets of shoe prints facing each other. Point out that one set of prints will represent the student and the other set of prints will represent the other person that is involved in the problem. Ask the student to stand in their own shoe prints first as they tell how they feel and what they think about the problem. Next ask them to step on the shoe prints of the other person. As they do this ask the student to become that person – thinking and feeling like them. Ask them now to share how they (actually the other person) might feel and think about the problem. Assist by "setting the scene" and asking questions. Process this activity pointing out if any new perspectives or understandings were revealed.

Handout:

PERSPECTIVES IN PROBLEM-SOLVING

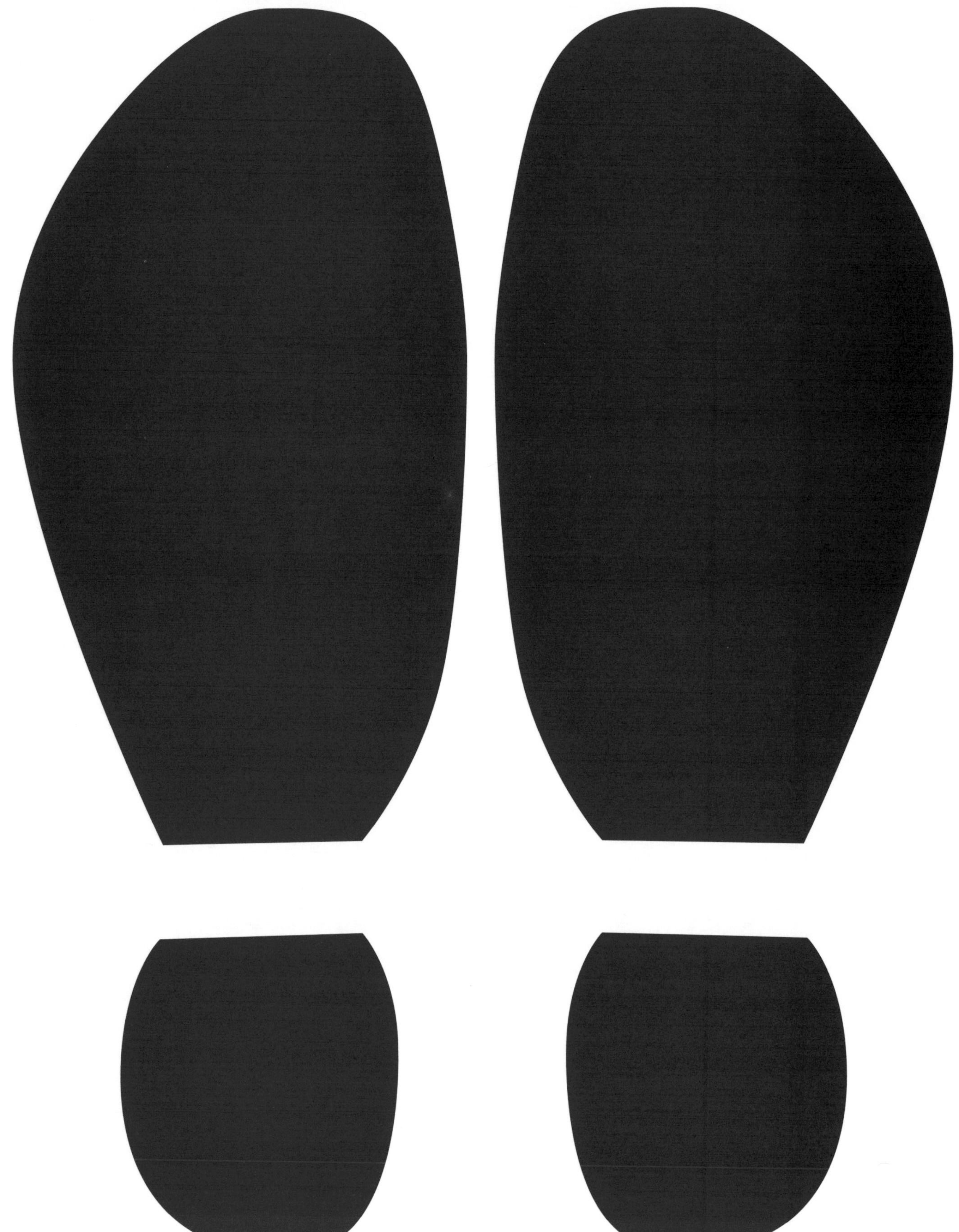

ATTITUDE*

Purpose: To help the child understand what an attitude is, how an attitude effects the problem, and empower them to realize that they are in charge of their attitude thus how they deal with their problem

Materials: Pair of large plastic, silly glasses with the lenses removed and a pair of three other sunglasses that have different colored lenses such as blue, red, and green often found at dollar or department stores. In place of store-bought glasses with different colored lenses, you may want to consider using cardboard glasses with different colored plastic wrap over them.

Procedure: Ask the student what comes to mind when they hear the word attitude. Point out that attitudes can be either negative or positive. Tell them there are 3 main words in the definition of attitude, encourage them to guess the three words which are THINK+FEEL=ACT. Often students are able to guess "feel" and "act or do" but they often omit the "think" word which is the most important for it is the one they have control over and it determines the attitude.

Compare the way we "think" about a situation to the way we "look at" a situation. Share the glasses as follows:

RED lenses – used when we "look at" a situation in an angry way
BLUE lenses – used when we "look at" a situation in a sad way
GREEN lenses – used when we "look at" a situation by denying or blaming others
LARGE CLEAR lenses – used to "look at" a situation clearly using our clear mind

Give examples of the messages that you are sending in your head with the different glasses – what you are saying to yourself about the situation. Examples of messages we may send in our head depending on our attitude are:

RED lenses – "How dare they do that. That's not fair."
BLUE lenses – "I'm no good. I can't do anything right."
GREEN lenses – "It wasn't my fault. He made me do it."
LARGE CLEAR lenses – "I am a good person. We all make mistakes at times, it's okay."

Role play different situations putting on the different glasses and sharing the "thinking." Always end with the CLEAR glasses and the clear thinking message.

Then use the presenting problem that the student is dealing with to apply the different glasses. Focus on the CLEAR glasses and the messages sent to the brain and the thoughts needed. Encourage the student to carry around their pretend pair of good attitude CLEAR glasses.

*original idea from Linda Myrick, Ph.D.

Activity:

PROBLEM-SOLVING WITH THE OKAY SIGNAL*

Purpose: To provide an approach to managing problems using the framework of finding an okay way to THINK, SAY, or something okay to DO to manage the problem in an okay way

Materials: *(Optional)* Copy the following Okay Signal Worksheet for the student to complete

Procedure: Form the okay signal with your hand and share with the student that this is just not any ordinary okay signal but a very special signal that will help with our problems. Proceed to tell them the three words on the upright fingers of THINK, SAY, and DO. Have them create their okay signal with their hand repeating the words as they touch those fingers. Explain that our special okay signal will help with the problem by encouraging us to find an okay way to THINK about the problem, or an okay way to SAY something to someone about the problem, or something that is okay to DO about the problem so we feel OKAY.

Encourage the student to restate the presenting problem and then together create okay ways to THINK, SAY, or DO about it. If a strategy of managing the problem is shared that is not appropriate then ask the student, "Is that an okay way to handle this problem?" Remind the student that it needs to follow the Okay rule.

You may choose to put the plan in writing by using the THINK, SAY, and DO Worksheet.

What can I THINK, SAY or DO that would help the problem?

*adapted with permission from Sitsch and Senn (2002). *Puzzle Pieces: The Classroom Guidance Connection.* Chapin, SC: YouthLight, Inc. www.youthlightbooks.com

OKAY SIGNAL Worksheet

The problem is ______________________________

____

____

I can find an OKAY way to THINK, SAY, or DO about my problem so I feel OKAY.

THINK ______________________________

____

____

THINK SAY DO

SAY ______________________________

____

____

____

____

DO ______________________________

____

____

____

THINK BUBBLE / TALK BUBBLE

Purpose: To provide a visual in structuring what to "think" or "say" to manage the problem

Materials: Copy, cut out, and if possible laminate the THINK BUBBLE and TALK BUBBLE on page 61

Procedure: After the problem has been defined, begin exploring positive ways to think about what may need to be said to cope with or manage the problem. Show the THINK BUBBLE and TALK BUBBLE. Refer to cartoon strips in which the bubbles indicate what the cartoon character may be saying or thinking. Demonstrate by holding the smaller bubbles leading to the large bubble beside your head and specify this as the THINK BUBBLE. Do the same with the arrow TALK BUBBLE and explain that this bubble shows what the person is saying.

Provide an overhead / erasable marker and have the student complete the bubbles and then demonstrate by holding the bubble beside his / her head and explaining the bubbles. Discuss how and when this could be thought or said, if the response is helpful, and possible consequences or outcomes.

THINK BUBBLE

TALK BUBBLE

REFRAME IT!*

Purpose: To assist the child to view the problem in a more positive way

Materials: Paper, pencil, crayons / markers, copy of the Picture Frames on pages 63 and 64 - cut out (don't forget to cut out the center), and laminate, if possible.

Procedure: After you have discussed and pinpointed the problem, ask the student to draw a picture of the problem on the paper.

FIRST: **Take the negative picture frame and place around the drawing. Begin talking together about the negative way you could choose to look at the problem.**

NEXT: **Reframe or replace the negative frame with the positive frame. Together talk about the positive way in which you could choose to look at the problem.**

THEN: **Ask them which frame would help them deal with the problem better. Ask which frame they would choose (emphasize the word choose or choice).**

If it is helpful to the child consider allowing the child to take the picture frame with them as a visual reminder to look at the positive in problems.

*adapted with permission from Senn (2003). *Small Group Counseling for Children, Grades 2-5.* Chapin, SC: YouthLight, Inc. www.youthlightbooks.com

Handout:
NEGATIVE FRAME

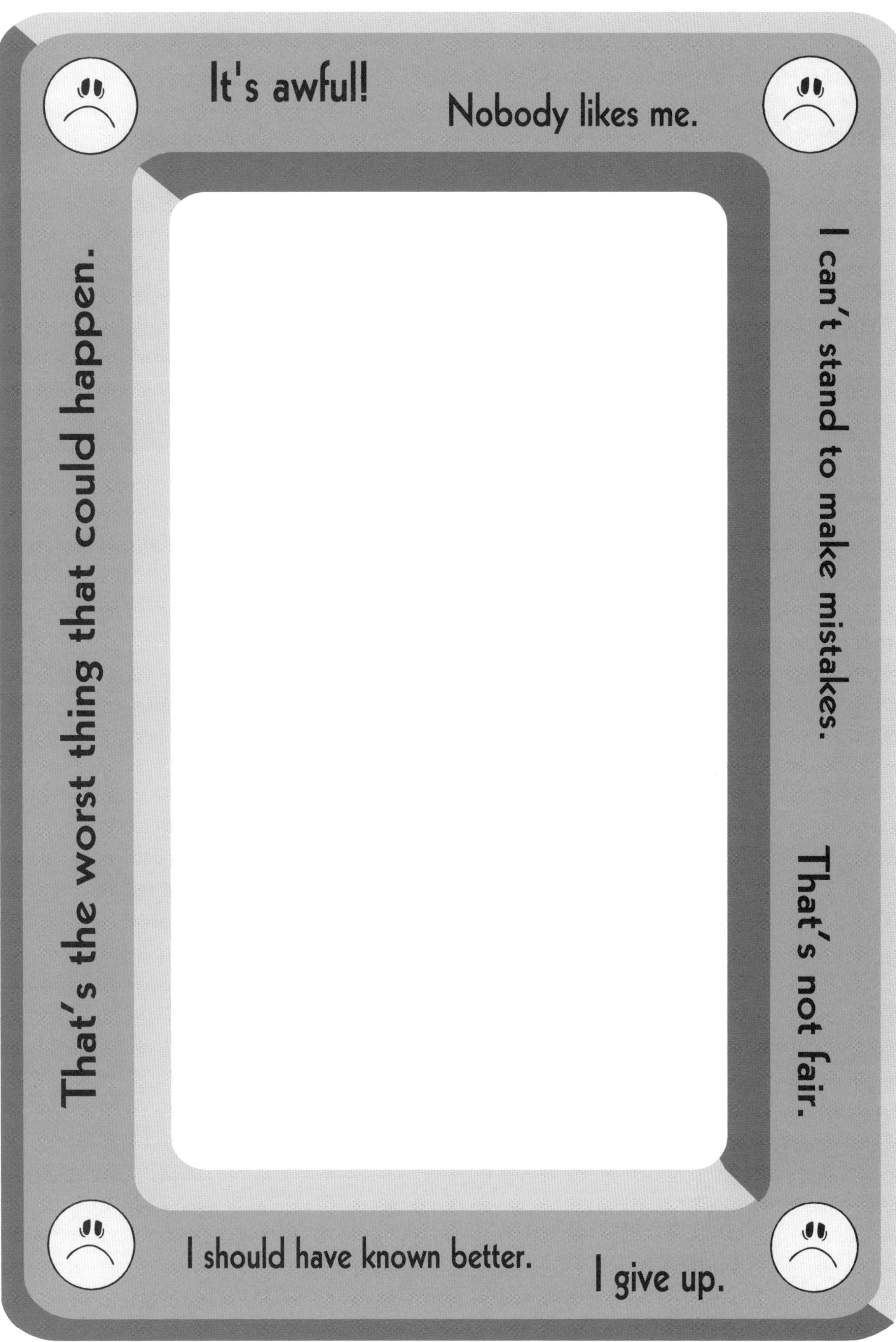

Handout:

POSITIVE FRAME

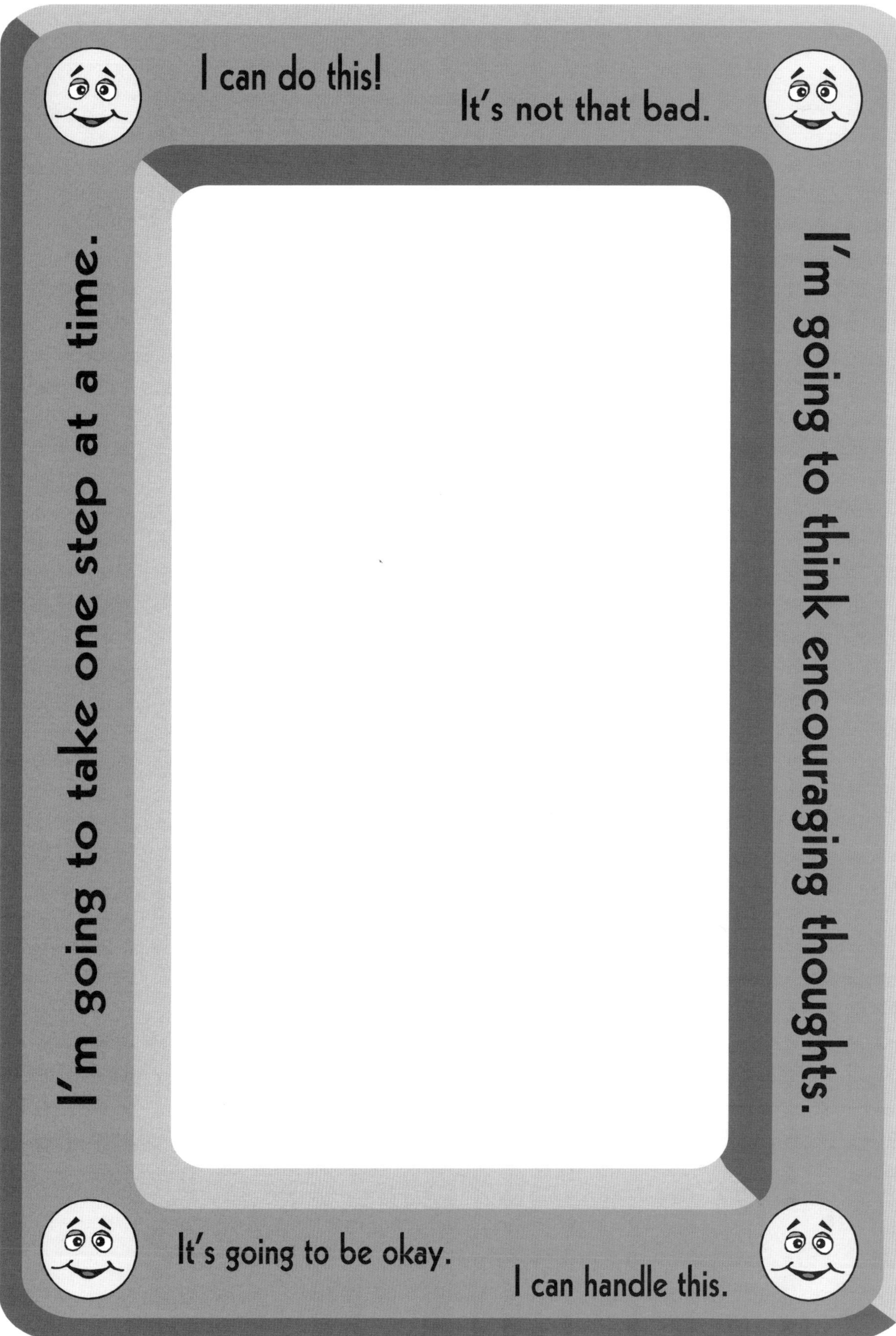

FEELINGS

This section deals with understanding, exploring, and dealing with the feelings that are a part of who we are and are a part of the problems we deal with. Being able to target our feelings is the building block necessary for learning to manage the feeling and the problem / situation. The four basic feelings are happy, mad, sad, scared.

The *FEELING EXPLORATIONS* part of this section provides activities to explore with the student different feelings, to begin to connect feelings to different situations, and to learn positive ways to manage or deal with those feelings.

Anger is one of our stronger emotions that seems to be a part of many situations in various forms. Anger and mad feelings are not bad, it is our reaction or response to the feeling that may be inappropriate. Feeling mad is unpleasant, but OK. It's what you do with the feeling that counts. This section includes *ANGER ACTIVITIES* to pinpoint and be aware of the feeling, to be aware of triggers and body cues associated with anger, to learn immediate anger reduction activities, and to learn rethinking/refocusing strategies to reduce the anger.

Feeling sad, at times, is a normal part of who we are, however when our sad feelings seem to dominate our life then we need to put things back into perspective. This section includes *SADNESS ACTIVITIES* to help deal with those sad feelings. The focus is on developing positive ways to think about the situation and manage the problem. Activities for focusing on helping others is also emphasized.

Anxieties, worries, and fears are a part of our lives. Children deal with developmental fears of the dark – "nighttime monsters," death, separation from parents, and stress from school/home/outside activities. In addition, our children are coping with increased media coverage of terrorism and natural disasters. This section provides *FEARS / ANXIETY ACTIVITIES* to address some of these issues.

Activity: FEELING TOSS

Purpose: To provide an active, game-like method to explore feelings

Materials: Create a poster size tic-tac-toe board. Add pictures of feeling faces (both pleasant and unpleasant) inside the squares of the tic-tac-toe board. You may choose to enlarge the feeling faces on pages 68-69 to use on the poster board. Need two bean bags or coins to toss on the squares.

Procedure: Discuss feelings by tossing the bean bag or coins on the different feeling faces. As the bean bag or coin lands on a square, take time to name the feeling and share an example when someone might feel that way. This works best if both the student and the counselor give examples. After playing several rounds, you may choose to add to the discussion appropriate strategies for dealing with the unpleasant feelings.

MUSICAL FEELINGS

Purpose: To creatively express feelings

Materials: Various musical instruments

Procedure: Display the musical instruments for the child and demonstrate how music can convey different feelings by playing an instrument with first a happy tune / rhythm, then next a sad tune / rhythm, then a scared tune / rhythm. Allow the student to choose an instrument to join you. Next take turns with a person playing a feeling and the other person guessing it. Then give an example of a situation that would have a strong feeling and have the person play what that feeling may be. The child can create his/her own situations and play the feeling. Take note of the situations the child shares and consider if it is pertinent to the presenting problem. Below are some feeling situations to get you started:

- How would you feel if someone were teasing you and called you a name?
- How would you feel if your parents said you could invite someone to spend the night?
- How would you feel if you had a bad dream?
- How would you feel if your friend ignored you?
- How would you feel if a friend complimented you on how well you played soccer?
- How would you feel if you made a bad grade on your Math test?
- How would you feel if you got an A on your Science project?

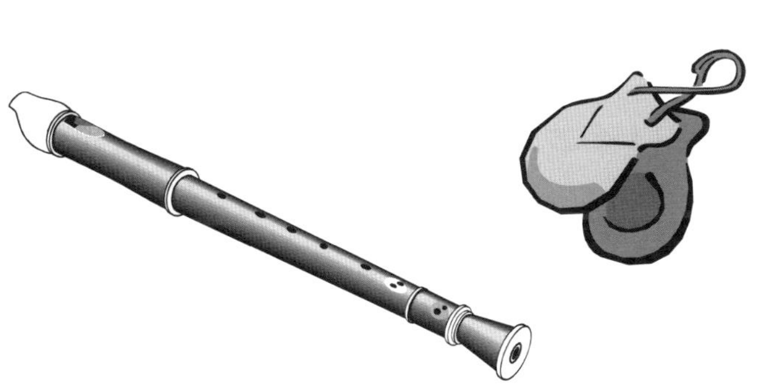

FACE YOUR FEELING

Purpose: To help the child communicate, through their body language (facial cues), what they are feeling and to be able to "read" others' body language more effectively

Materials: Mirror, pictures of children with different feeling faces copied and cut apart. You may even ask a student who has good facial expressions to pose for you to take different feeling pictures with a camera.

Procedure: Show the feeling face pictures discussing what he / she sees in the face that can indicate the feeling. Point out the eyebrows, the gaze of the eyes, any wrinkles on the face, the tilt of the head, and the look of the mouth. Ask the child to make the same face and then look in the mirror to check the accuracy of the facial features. Give examples of feeling situations. Take turns making the feeling faces while the other person guesses the feeling. Discuss how knowing and expressing your feelings as well as guessing how someone else might be feeling can help in getting along with that person. For example, ask, "If a friend was playing with the trucks on the floor, and you came and picked up one of the trucks, and he looked up with an angry face - what might that tell you about what's going on and what you should do?"

Handout:

FEELING FACES

EXCITED

HAPPY

PROUD

CONFUSED

SHY

BORED

Activity: FEELING WHEEL*

Purpose: To understand the basic feelings of happy, mad, sad, afraid, shy, and proud and to find helpful strategies for dealing with the feeling

Materials: Copy the Feeling Wheel Sheets (pages 72 and 73), fastening brad, scissors, and crayons

Procedure: Share the feeling faces on the first wheel. Allow time to discuss, giving examples of a time the child may have felt that way. Point out that all feelings are okay and normal to have but that we have to learn to manage our unpleasant feelings in an okay way.

Give an example of a helpful and unhelpful way to manage our feelings. Then brainstorm together the strategies to help manage our feelings in helpful ways. Next, show the "what to do" wheel and discuss the strategies shown for appropriate ways to handle unpleasant feelings.

Assist the child in assembling their Feeling Wheel – add color to the pictures if time allows. Demonstrate how it works (see directions "For Use" on the Feeling Wheel sheet). Share some of the following situations asking the child to turn their arrow pointing to how they might feel in the situation and then turning the wheel to choose a helpful way to manage the feeling. Allow time to share and discuss. Feeling situations are:

- **How would you feel if someone teases you?**
- **How would you feel if you were the new person in the classroom?**
- **How would you feel if you studied hard for a test and made an "A?"**
- **How would you feel if your pet ran away?**
- **How would you feel if you were pushed out of line?**

You may choose to involve the parents by sending the note on the following page.

*adapted with permission from Senn (2004). *Small Group Counseling for Children Grades K-2.* Chapin, SC: YouthLight, Inc. www.youthlightbooks.com

Handout:
FEELING WHEEL- Parent Note

Dear Parent,

Today when I talked with your child in our counseling session we focused on the feelings of happy, sad, mad, scared, proud, and shy. We emphasized that ALL feelings are okay and normal however we need to find good ways to handle and be in control of our feelings.

Your child completed a feeling wheel that provides a system to identify the feeling in the situation and then make choices about what to do to handle the feeling appropriately. Spend time role-playing and practicing with your child how to use the wheel and then direct your child to use the wheel to help in real life situations. To use the Feeling Wheel when a situation arises: First help your child decide what he/she may be feeling. Instruct your child to turn the arrow to that feeling face. Next, look at the smaller inside wheel and together decide which strategy may be a helpful way to handle the feeling. Turn the "What to do" strategy to the feeling to line up the feeling, arrow, and strategy. Encourage your child to follow through with the chosen strategy, sharing compliments and encouragements.

Thank you for your help in working together for the success of the child.

Sincerely,

Your School Counselor

Handout:

FEELING WHEEL

Directions: Copy and cut out the two circles and the arrow on pages 72-73. Then assemble with the larger circle on the bottom, the smaller circle next, and the arrow on top. Insert a brad through the centers to hold the circles and arrow together.

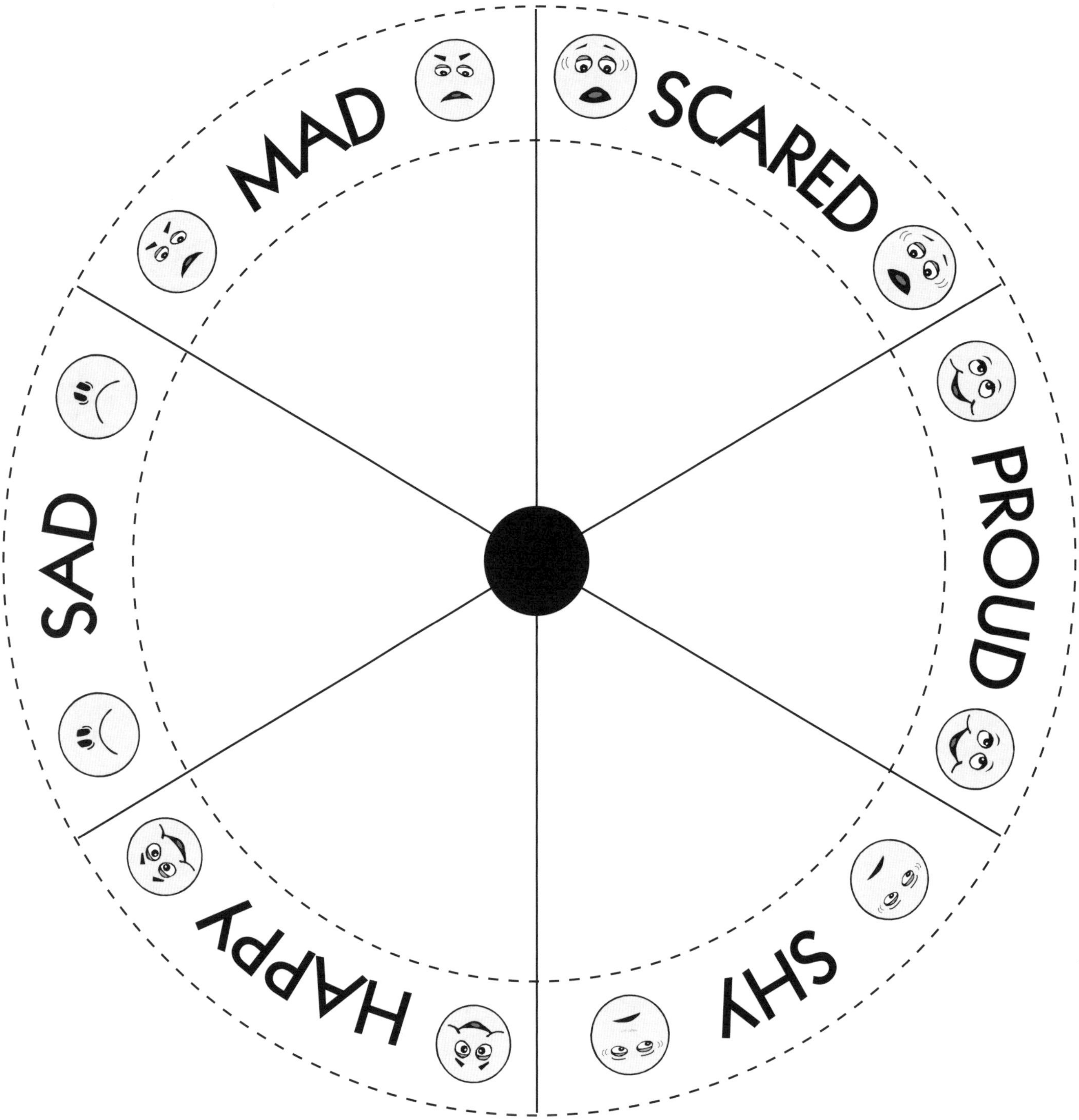
MAD
SCARED
PROUD
SHY
HAPPY
SAD

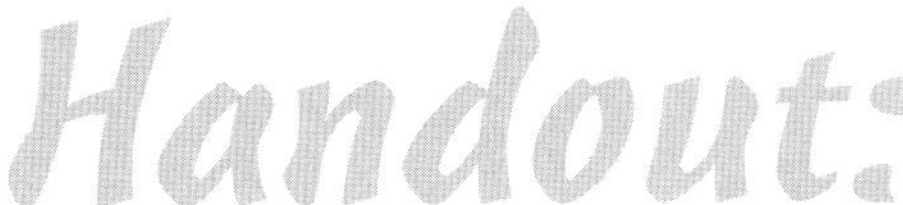

Handout:
FEELING WHEEL

Directions: When there is a situation, decide what you are feeling and turn the arrow to the feeling face. Next, look at the smaller inner circle and decide which may be a helpful way to handle the feeling. Then, turn the "What To Do" strategy to the feeling to line up the feeling, arrow, and strategy.

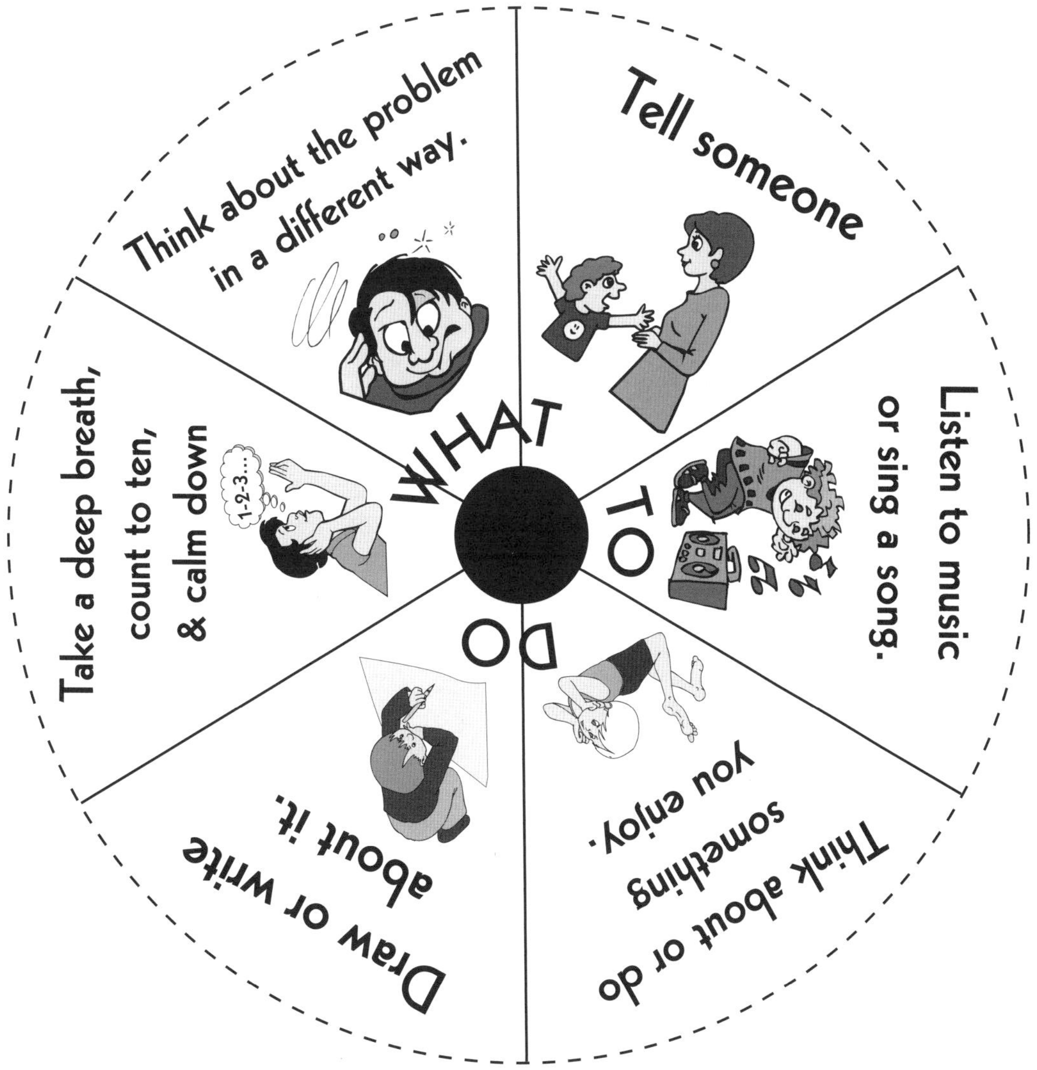

WHAT TO DO
Tell someone
Listen to music or sing a song.
Think about or do something you enjoy.
Draw or write about it.
Take a deep breath, count to ten, & calm down
1-2-3...
Think about the problem in a different way.

Feelings

Activity:

FEELINGS BEHIND THE MASK

Purpose: To encourage students to communicate his/her real feelings so he/she can effectively help and deal with the situation

Materials: A mask – may choose to use a Halloween mask (a non-scary mask) or just create a mask from poster board drawing a regular face of a person

Procedure: Hold the mask up to your face and behind the mask make a feeling face asking the student to guess the feeling. Allow the student to hold the mask up making the feeling face behind the mask as you guess the feeling. Point out that it could only be a total guess as to the feeling because of the mask and that it would take longer to help with the feelings because of the mask. Share that there may be times that we hide our feelings by smiling and pretending everything is fine.

Discuss when and where it is important to show your true feelings.

Discuss how we can share our feelings with other caring people.

Activity: ANGER TRIGGERS

Purpose: To explore the types of things / situations about which we choose to get angry

Materials: Copy the Anger Triggers Worksheet

Procedure: Explore with the student typical situations that may cause the student to repeatedly get angry. Present possible situations with the following questions:

- **Problem in getting along with friends?**
- **When parents, teachers, or someone in authority is telling you to do or not do something?**
- **Do you get angry with class work or homework?**
- **With brother or sister?**

Encourage the student to complete the Anger Triggers worksheet listing 3 things that may bother him / her at the different levels.

As you review the information, begin to look at helping the student be aware of these triggers and to choose to rethink or redirect the situation to reduce the feeling of anger.

Worksheet:

ANGER TRIGGERS

Directions: Think of the things you get angry about. Look at the thermometer that indicates the different levels showing the degree of anger. It ranges from bothered to boiling mad. Think of 3 typical situations or things that can happen for each level that describe the levels of anger that you feel.

BOILING MAD

1. ______________________

____

2. ______________________

____

3. ______________________

____

MAD

1. ______________________

____

2. ______________________

____

3. ______________________

____

BOTHERED or ANNOYED

1. ______________________

____

2. ______________________

____

3. ______________________

____

CALM DOWN with the ROLL of the DICE

Purpose: To tune-in to our body signals when we first begin to feel angry so we can begin anger-reduction techniques.

Materials: Dice, pencil, and a copy of the Calm Down with the Roll of the Dice Worksheet

Procedure: Ask the student to think about what happens to his / her body when he / she gets really angry. Ask if he / she has ever noticed their body reacting to anger in the following way(s):

- Breathing faster
- Clenched fist(s)
- Clenched jaw
- Face becomes hot / red
- Butterflies in the stomach
- Thinking shuts down
- Pounding heart
- Tightness in the chest

Help the student understand that when our body starts to react to being mad we need to calm down and get in control so that we do not make things worse. Catching our anger on the beginning and claming down is easier than dealing with our anger when we have reached the "boiling point."

Ask the student to think of a time that he / she has been really angry and yet was able to calm down and get his / her anger under control. Make a list of the appropriate ways to calm down and manage the anger. The list may include:

- Talk to an adult or friend you trust
- Do something active like play basketball, jog, or jump rope
- Write the problem down and think it through
- Walk away from the problem
- Distract yourself by doing something fun
- Remind yourself of the consequences for anger out of control
- Take several deep breaths
- Count to 10
- Listen to music
- Imagine a peaceful place
- Tell yourself to calm down

Tell the student to select his / her top six ways to calm down to manage the anger and add these to the Calm Down with the Roll of the Dice Activity Sheet.

Role-play with the student situations that trigger anger. Use the following steps for each role-play.

STEP 1: Describe the situation that you are getting angry about.
STEP 2: Describe the reaction of your body to the anger.
STEP 3: Roll the dice and use the anger-reduction strategy that corresponds to the number on the dice.
STEP 4: Describe how your body now feels and what you are thinking.

Allow the student to take their sheet and dice with them to use in real-life situations.

Worksheet:

CALM DOWN with the Roll of the DICE

Directions: Write or draw a picture of an anger-reduction technique in each of the dice boxes below.

For Use: When you begin to feel angry, roll the dice and use the anger-reduction technique that corresponds to the number on the dice.

Activity:

TRAFFIC LIGHT*

Purpose: To learn and practice implementing an anger-reduction technique

Materials: Materials to create a green / yellow / red traffic light on paper

Procedure: Discuss anger with the student and the importance of gaining control of the angry feeling. Assist the student to create a traffic light on paper that can be used to practice and role play gaining control of the angry feelings and then can be used in "real life" situations.

Give the student the following directions for reducing anger by using the traffic light:

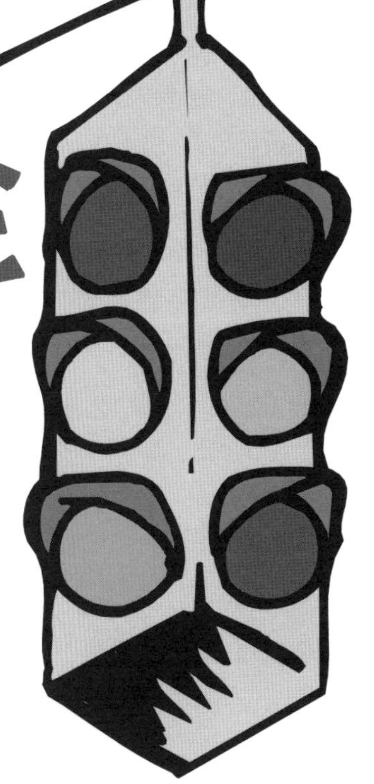

1. When you begin to get angry, place your finger on the red light for two or three minutes. Keep your finger there until the worst of the anger is under control.

2. Next, put your finger on the yellow light for at least two minutes. Think about what made you angry. Review how you handled yourself. Ask yourself if there was anything that you could have thought or done differently. If you need to write a plan for improvement do so.

3. Finally, place your finger on the green light for two minutes. Compliment yourself for gaining control of your anger. Take a deep breath and return to your work or play.

*adapted with permission from T. Carr (2000). *131 Creative Strategies for Reaching Children with Anger Problems.* Chapin, SC: YouthLight, Inc. www.youthlightbooks.com

SAND TIMER

Purpose: To learn and practice implementing an anger-reduction technique

Materials: Minute sand timer (or use the sand timer from the *Chill Out Bag* available through www.youthlightbooks.com)

Procedure: Discuss anger – how our body feels, what we say or do when we are angry. Acknowledge with the student that feeling mad is normal and how we choose to deal with our anger is important – we need to look for healthy, appropriate ways to deal with the feeling.

Introduce the use of the sand timer. Share that when we are mad we can choose to focus on the sand dropping while we take deep breaths and tell ourselves to calm down. By allowing ourselves to calm, we give time for our brain to turn on so we can find a good way to deal with the feeling.

Role-play an angry situation, allowing the student to practice turning the sand timer upside down, taking deep breaths and calming down. If you have extra sand timers you may choose to allow the student to borrow one to use when needed.

Activity: SCREAM BAG

Purpose: To provide a creative way to release anger

Materials: Brown bag – lunch bag size (or scream sack from the *Chill Out Bag* available through www.youthlightbooks.com), crayon / markers

Procedure: Together decorate a scream bag that can be used to scream into to release anger. Talk about how it is not okay to "scream" at a person or say mean things to hurt them but that it may help to scream into a bag to get out the extra angry energy. Allow time to role-play the scream bag in action.

SCREAM BOX

Purpose: To provide a creative strategy for anger release

Materials: Empty shoe box, construction paper, old newspaper, empty toilet paper roll, markers, scissors, and glue.

Procedure: A completed scream box is for the purpose of screaming into to release angry energy – better than screaming at a person or saying mean things. If the student likes hands-on activities, then the process of making the scream box may be helpful to remind the student to find appropriate ways to deal with anger.

To make a scream box, cut a hole in the middle of the lid of an empty shoe box for the empty toilet paper roll to fit – tape this together. Next stuff the inside of the box with old newspapers. Place the top on the box and decorate the outside with construction paper and designs.

Practice using the scream box by role-playing an angry situation and then screaming into the box through the top of the toilet paper roll. The paper inside absorbs the sound, doesn't bother others and yet allows for release of angry energy.

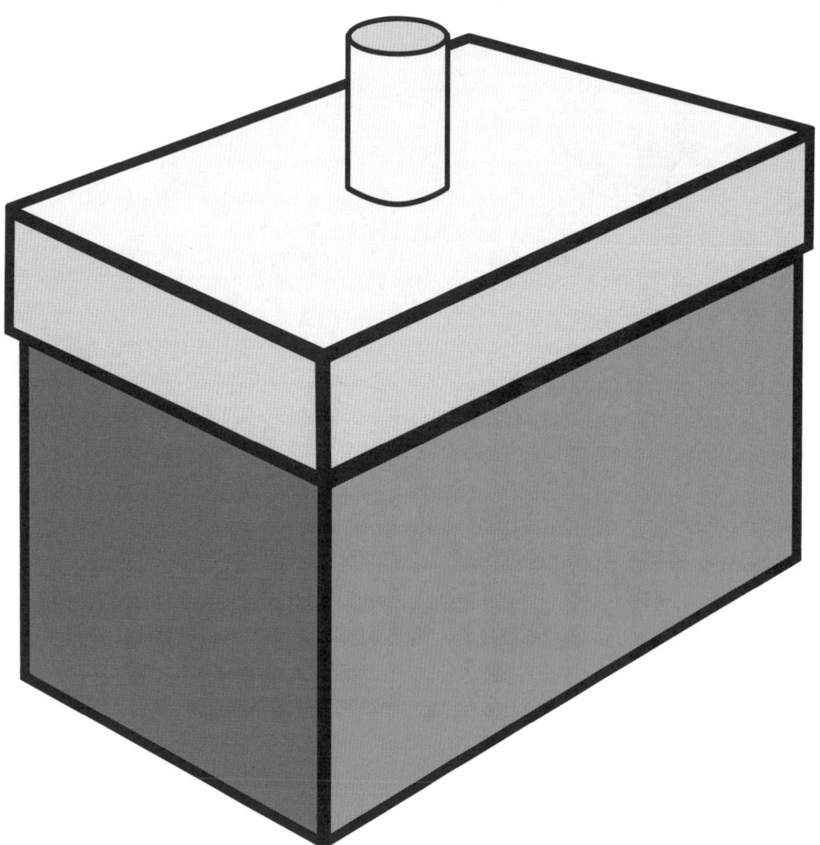

Activity: SNAP, CRACKLE, POP

Purpose: To release angry energy in an appropriate way

Materials: Bubble wrap and packing noodles

Procedure: It's good to have packing noodles and bubble wrap on hand for students to use as an anger release. Allow the student to tear up packing noodles and pop bubble wrap rather than hurting others or property.

Activity:

RUBBER BAND FLEXIBILITY

Purpose: To emphasize the importance of flexibility in situations

Materials: Rubber band

Procedure: Ask the student if they always get their way? Talk about what happens if they insist on always having their own way and do not ever bend or change. Present the importance of bending, being willing to change, or being flexible with the situation.

Show the rubber band and demonstrate how it expands and contracts depending on the needs – it would be ineffective if it were not flexible.

Encourage the student to be willing to change the way he/she is thinking about something or to be willing to change the plans when needed.

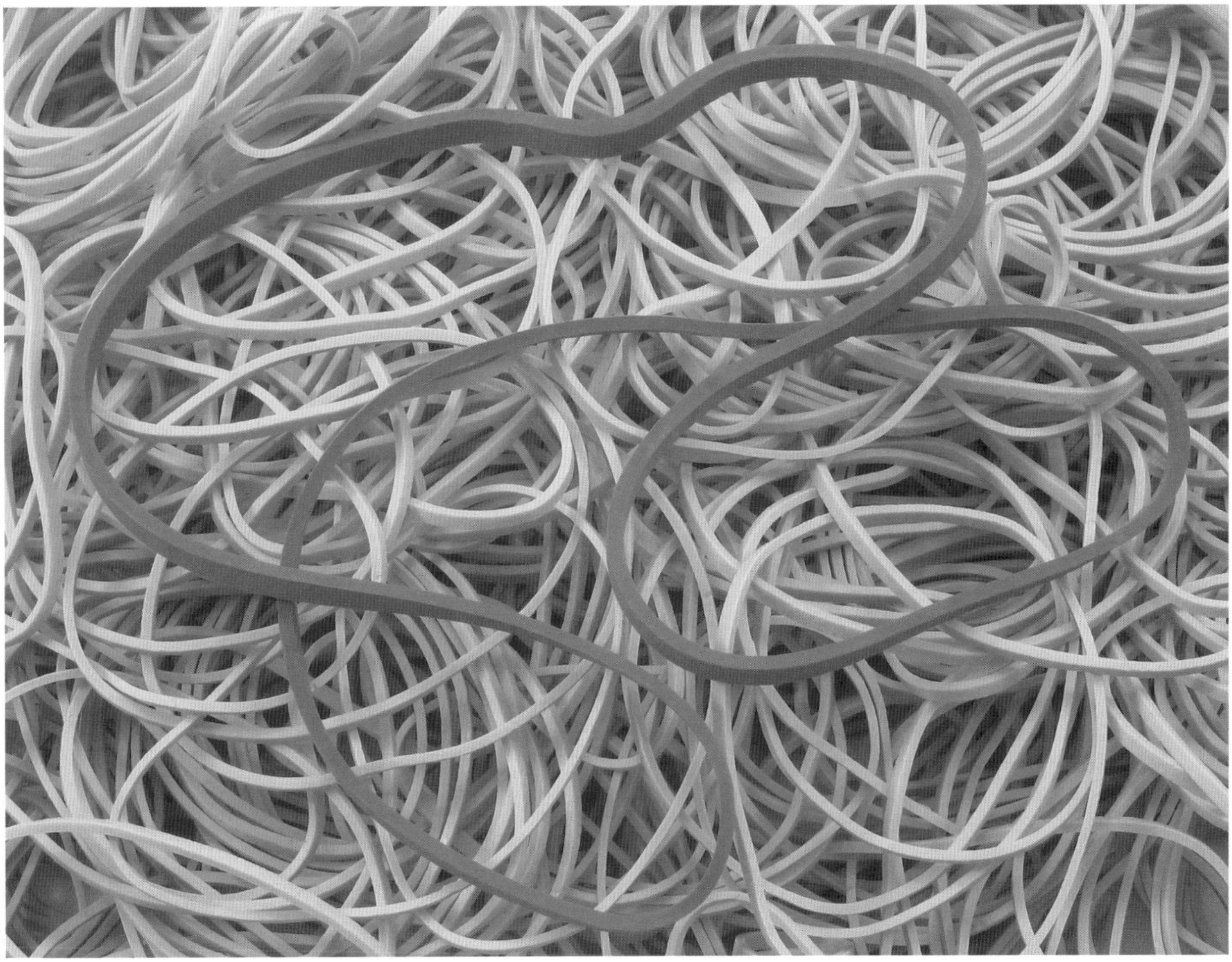

Activity: ANGER SURVIVAL KIT

Purpose: To provide hands-on items for the child for anger management

Materials: Box or bag and other items you choose for the kit

Procedure: The child can create their own "Anger Survival Kit" to take with them by making the items in the prior listed activities of: Sand Timer, Scream Bag, Scream Box, Packing Noodles and Bubble Wrap, and Rubber Band Flexibility. Place the items you choose in a box or bag labeled "Anger Survival Kit."

Practice with the student regarding when and how to use the items in the kit to help with anger management.

ROLLER COASTER*

Purpose: To provide strategies for combating the "lows" of life

Materials: Copy of the Roller Coaster Worksheet for the student to complete

Procedure: Begin a discussion about roller coasters, explain that an exciting roller coaster is usually filled with highs and lows, ups and downs. Share that "life is like a roller coaster." Explain by comparing the highs and lows of life to the highs and lows of a roller coaster. Give examples of feelings that we experience when we are at or building to a high and those that we experience when we are at or going to a low.

Give the student the Roller Coaster Sheet. Call out some life events and have him / her point on the roller coaster, either a high or low or in-between, to indicate where their feelings would be.

- Someone teases you because your clothes are not "cool."
- You overhear your parents bragging about something you did.
- You forget your homework.
- You win a science prize.
- Your pet is lost.
- Your parents tell you they are getting a divorce.
- You get to spend the night with a friend.
- A loved one dies.

Ask the student to complete the part of the sheet listing 2 highs and 2 lows in his / her life.

Explain that when the coaster is at a low, it must work hard to get back up to the high. Many students who have ridden a roller coaster will be able to describe how the coaster feels as it is pulling itself up the hill. The same is true for us – when we are low, we must work hard to get back "up." Refer to the bottom of the sheet, pointing out the suggestions for getting back up. Read the suggestions and have the student add some of his / her own.

Caution the student about doing harmful or negative things to get back up (drugs, gangs, etc.) Discuss how these "quick fixes" only take you lower because after the "high" you have two problems with which to deal: the original problem and the problem of using drugs (or alcohol, or breaking the law, etc.)

*adapted with permission from Sitsch and Senn, (2002). *Puzzle Pieces: The Classroom Guidance Connection*. Chapin, SC: YouthLight, Inc. www.youthlightbooks.com

ROLLER COASTER

We all have HIGHS and LOWS. Write two of each of yours below:

HIGHS	**LOWS**
1. ______________________	1. ______________________
______________________	______________________
2. ______________________	2. ______________________
______________________	______________________

Directions: When you are at a low point, you will need to do something to help you feel better. Here are some ideas. Use the blank lines to write four ideas of your own.

Talk to someone you trust

Write a letter to yourself stating all the great things about you

Go visit a neighbor who needs cheering up

Dance

Play with your pet

Exercise

____

____

____

____

HALF FULL / HALF EMPTY

Purpose: To encourage the choice to view life optimistically rather then pessimistically

Materials: A glass of water half filled with water

Procedure: Show the glass of water and ask the student if the glass is half full or half empty. Explore the correct answer until you come to the conclusion that both answers are correct it just depends on how you look at it – the choice you make.

Share the following story:

The first child was asked by his parents to go out and pull the weeds out of the flower garden. It was a very hot summer day with the sun beaming down. The child's mom brought out this half filled glass of water and in a complaining voice the child said, "Gee mom, why did you bring me a half empty glass of water? Don't you know how hot it is out here? Why couldn't you bring me more?"

The second child was asked by his parents to go out and pull the weeds out of the flower garden. It was very hot outside with the sun beaming down. This child's mom brought out this half filled glass of water and the child said, "Thanks mom, I sure needed some water. Thank you."

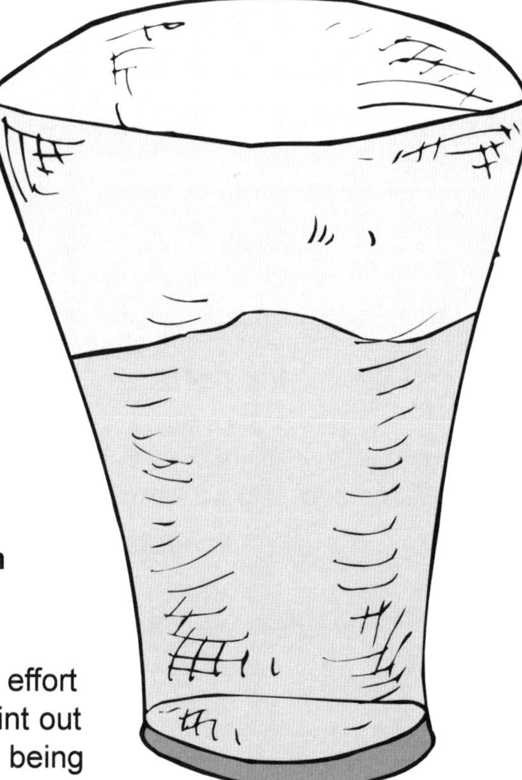

We can be happy about what we have or complain about it. Ask:

- **Which child do you think will be happier in life?**
- **How do you get to be the "half full" kind of person who looks at the bright side of things?**

Come to the conclusion that it is our choice and it may take effort and energy to get into the habit but we will be happier. Point out that things will happen to us that we don't like – our friend being mean to us, not getting to do something we have really been wanting to do, failing a test, etc. but that it is our choice in the attitude we have about the situation. Talk about messages you can send to your brain, ways to think, and how to look for the positives in each situation.

Activity: DARK CLOUDS / RAYS OF SUNSHINE

Purpose: To identify and replace thoughts that are unhealthy for us

Materials: Copy and cut out the dark clouds and the rays of sunshine on pages 90 and 91

Procedure: Review the Dark Clouds and Rays of Sunshine Worksheet together. Review the unhealthy thoughts of the dark clouds and then match the better way of thinking listed on the sunshine rays.

Ask the student to identify any dark cloud thoughts he/she may use and then help the student rewrite to healthier thoughts on the sunshine ray.

Handout:

DARK CLOUDS

DEMANDING

- I just have to win.
- I can't make a mistake.

MAGNIFYING

- If I have to get up in front of the class it will be horrible.

COPPING OUT

- I couldn't get my homework done because they were watching TV.
- I would get a better grade if the teacher wasn't so mean.
- He made me do it.

OVER-GENERALIZING

- I always get into trouble.
- He never has to help.
- She gets all of the attention.

Handout:

RAYS OF SUNSHINE

Instead of DEMANDING think "It's OK if..." or "I would really like it if..."

Instead of MAGNIFYING think "It will be embarrassing, but I'll survive."

Instead of COPPING OUT think "It's up to me to..." or "I'm the one who will need to..."

Instead of OVER-GENERALIZING think "Sometimes it seems like... but..."

Activity: SELF-TALK COMPUTER STYLE

Purpose: To utilize self-talk to replace negative thoughts with positive thoughts

Materials: Assess to a word processing program on a computer

Procedure: Explain to the student that self-talk is what we say to ourselves – what we think in our brain – the message we type into our brain's computer.

Use the analogy of typing on the computer to our brain by explaining that if we make a mistake in the typing or don't like the sentence we first write we can either backspace or delete and then replace with the right information. Point out that our thoughts are like that too. We can either fill the brain with junk thoughts about things we are not good at or things that did not go well but we also can choose to fill our brain with good thoughts about ourselves and things we can do well.

Ask the student to go to the computer and type out positive statements about themselves and what they can do well. (If they appear to be heavily focusing on the negative have them first type a negative message and then use the delete button to get rid of it!)

Activity: SELFLESS ACTS

Purpose: To move the focus from ourselves - our wants and needs - to the focus on the needs of others

Materials: Copy the Acts of Kindness Assignment Worksheet

Procedure: Discuss how it feels to do something nice for others. Ask the student to share examples of kind things they may have done in the past. Ask their assistance to help others by accepting an "Acts of Kindness" assignment.

Create the assignment together by completing the "Acts of Kindness Assignment" slip. Assignments may include such things as: complimenting a classmate, playing with someone who is alone at recess, sending a thank you note to your parent or teacher for something they have done, or doing something extra nice for a brother or sister.

Don't forget to follow-up with the assignment, processing the thoughts and feelings involved.

Worksheet:

ACTS OF KINDNESS ASSIGNMENT

I, ______________________________ plan to

____

____

I will say / do ______________________________

____

____

______________________ ______________________

Date Assigned Date to be Completed

HOW DID IT GO?

What do you think they thought or felt about your act of kindness?

____

____

What do you think or feel about having done the kind act?

____

____

GET THE FACTS
Separation Anxiety

Purpose: To gather information concerning why the child is upset and reluctant to come to school

Procedure: Dealing with the separation anxiety of a human being can be very complicated. Each person is different – reacting differently and needing different approaches. I wish there was one simple strategy to use that would help all students but there's no such strategy – what I will do is share different approaches and strategies that you can pull from to see which is helpful.

With separation anxiety it is important first to clarify the origin of the tears and reluctance to come to school. Is it just missing home and parents or is there something wrong at school, such as being picked on, etc. or maybe something wrong at home that they feel they need to be there to protect someone. It is important to check with teachers and parents to gain their insights as to what may be going on for the child. It is challenging to understand answers at times from a crying child and the typical "what's wrong?" kind of question doesn't always get a clear answer. I have found that using a MULTIPLE CHOICE QUESTION can help this process, such as:

I see you're upset. Are you upset because:

1.) Someone is bothering you at school and it scares you?

2.) You're missing mom or dad – being at home?

3.) The work is hard and it worries you that you don't understand the work?

4.) Something else?

I usually hold up my fingers and point to a finger as I say each possible choice, so they have a visual. Many times this allows the child to focus on figuring out the answer and helps them settle. Of course use different possibilities for 1-4 if you have other insights as to what might be the problem. The next step depends on the answer. If the answer is "missing mom or dad – home" then review the following activities to see if one may help.

TV CHANNEL CHANGER
Separation Anxiety

Purpose: To help redirect the child's thinking from missing home to participating in school

Procedure: Ask the child if they watch TV at home. Ask the student what he/she does if they don't like a channel they are watching – they turn the channel to something else. Relate that our thoughts in our head are like a TV, if what we are thinking is causing us to get upset then we need to switch to a different channel and think about something else.

Ask them to share some things about school that may be okay and fun to do. Together decide where their brain channel changer button is. They can then use this button to switch from missing home to thinking about something okay at school. Some examples of brain channel changer buttons can be the nose, tug on the ear, your elbow, etc. Role-play using the button.

MESSAGES...
Separation Anxiety

Purpose: To be the liaison at school between child and parent

Procedure: In talking with an upset child, one possible strategy is to offer to the child to get a message to their parent from them, however this is offered with certain stipulations. Ask the child what he/she would like for you to tell the parent. (If they say something like, "Tell my mom to come get me." I usually answer with, "I'll be glad to tell her you asked but I'm guessing your mom already knows you need to be here at school.") Use your counseling skills to be a good listener, summarizing and clarifying the information. Explain that as soon as they are in their class and participating then you can go call the parent. Explain that after you talk with the parent you can come back and share with them what the parent said.

You may choose to add:

For some students when I bring a message from their parent they get all upset again and it makes things worse but for other students my bringing a message back helps them be okay and they say, "Thank you." Which student do you think you are? Will bringing the message help or hurt?

Option: Allow and encourage the student to bring a picture of the parent from home. Allow the student to keep the picture with them and glance at it at different times with the message in their mind that the parent is always with them.

HOME CHECK CHART
Separation Anxiety

Purpose: To provide support and strategies to the parent regarding separation anxiety

Procedure: Contact with the parent is important. Often the parent is distraught over leaving a crying child at school, therefore a phone call is appreciated to let them know their child is in class and okay. Helping the parent understand that being consistent in bringing them to school each day and developing a routine are important. A Home Check Chart can be suggested in which the parent can create a chart adding the morning routine including things that they are successful with (such as gets dressed, brushes teeth etc.) as well as the difficult "walking into school with an okay face." The chart can help the child focus on challenges / successes of earning a sticker / star for the items and can help smooth the transition. Encourage the parent to give the chart a try. Also in your talk with the parent you can perhaps gain insight as to the parent/child interactions. Use your counseling skills as you compliment those interactions that are helpful and you provide alternative approaches for the interactions that may not be as helpful.

Activity:

SCHOOL CHECK CHART
Separation Anxiety

Purpose: To provide a visual strategy / incentive to help with the student's separation anxiety

Procedure: Consult with the teacher about the idea of creating a check chart for the student including such items as: coming into the classroom nicely, putting up bookbag, beginning morning work, cooperating – being a part of the group, etc. Smiley faces, stars, or earning points for a prize may work as an incentive. The chart can help the child focus on challenges / successes of earning a sticker/star for the items and can help smooth the transition.

WORRY ROCK

Purpose: To help define "worry" and healthy strategies to deal with worry

Materials: Rock, marker

Procedure: Explore the concept of worry through such questions as:

- **What does it mean to worry?**
- **What kinds of things might people worry about?**
- **What is something that you worry about? Is worrying helpful or not?**

Bring out in the discussion that when a person has a problem and he/she is not thinking about a solution or way to manage the problem then it is called "worrying" and it becomes a waste of time. Instead we need to find ways to get rid of the worry and find healthy ways to deal with the problem.

Propose that one way to get rid of our worry is to give it to the worry rock. Hold out a rock and proceed to tell the rock all of the worries. You may choose to write the worries on the rock with a marker.

Next choose one worry and focus the discussion on being a problem solver. Discuss ways to solve or manage the problem.

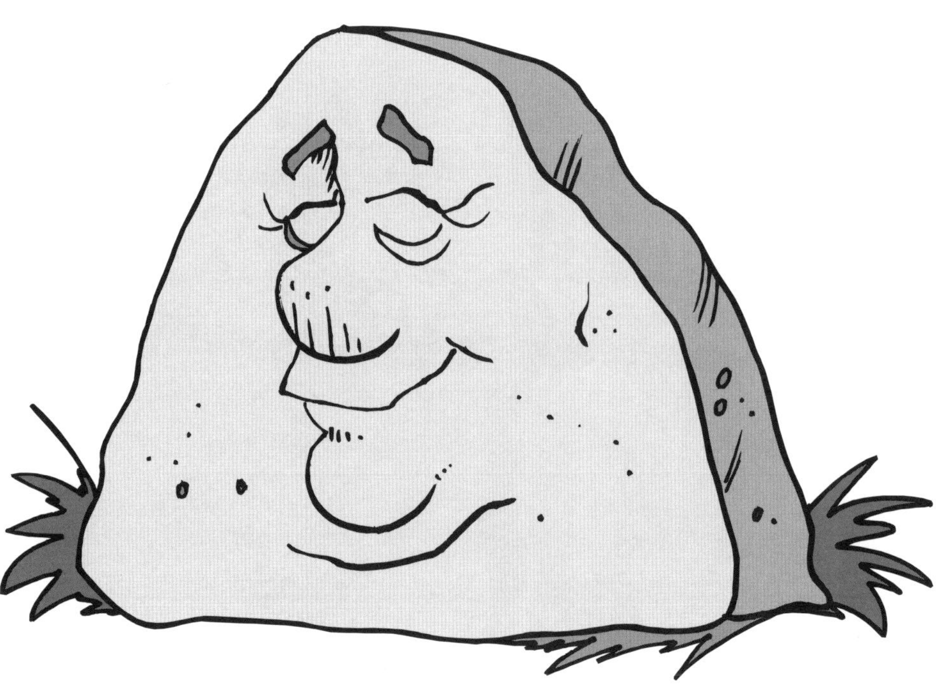

FEELING OVERWHELMED...

Purpose: To reduce the feeling of being overwhelmed

Materials: Paper and pencil

Procedure: Together review and write down all of the tasks / jobs of the student. Next prioritize the list marking those of most importance. Then add a time frame by each job that you "guesstamate" the time it will take you to complete. Finally make a plan for completing each – using a weekly calendar may be of help. This process helps the student to be in control thus reducing the overwhelmed feelings. If all of the jobs on the list are not "doable" discuss which jobs could be dropped or who else can be involved to help.

NIGHTTIME MONSTERS
Biblio-Counseling

Purpose: To utilize biblio-counseling to address nighttime worries of bad dreams and make-believe monsters

Materials: The storybook *How to Get Rid of Bad Dreams* by Nancy Hazbry and Roy Condy

Procedure: If a child is having bad dreams or is worried of make-believe monsters in the dark, there are many good children's books that can be used to open a discussion of this topic as well as gain strategies to help the child. In the book, *How to Get Rid of Bad Dreams,* the author talks about using a shrink-ray laser to shrink the monster, a mirror to hold up in front of the monster to scare him so he'll turn and run the other way, or a bottle of reducing potion to use on yourself to sneak away. The book not only provides funny ways to make bad dreams and make-believe scary monsters disappear but it also gives the child the power to conquer these fears. Brainstorm with the child ways he/she can use his/her "powers" to conquer the monsters.

TERRORISM and NATURAL DISASTERS

Purpose: To help the child deal with disasters beyond their control

Procedure: For students who have actually experienced a natural disaster or have been victims of a terrorist act, utilize your counseling skills as they share their story. Reflect their feelings, clarify and summarize, and most of all reinforce the strategies they may have used to handle the situation well. Assess the extent of trauma incurred and treat as Post Traumatic Stress Disorder if needed – refer out if appropriate.

If the student is worried or anxious about natural disasters or a terrorist act that others have suffered, begin by using your counseling skills to listen to the student share their concerns / worries. This will help gain an understanding of their perspective and their information. Compliment the student on being very caring and concerned. Focus the discussion on what he/she can do to help others - letters, donations, etc. The words from the American Red Cross can be helpful here, "There is one force more powerful than Mother Nature and that is Human Nature." Emphasize how we as caring people can come together to help each other. If the student expresses that they are worried about the disaster happening to them review safety rules and how to prepare to best deal with a problem.

In consulting with parents regarding the child's anxiety, the following excerpt on terrorism from Tip Frank's book, *The Handbook for Helping Kids with Anxiety and Stress.* * may be of help to share.

Suggestion: Parents and other adults need to limit exposure to the media. Kids are often exposed to situations and details through the media with which they are unable to cope. Try these three ideas.

a. Give kids the basic facts. Reduce T.M.I. (too much information)

b. Process what has happened while allowing kids to express their feelings. Listen well. Summarize and clarify what the child is saying and reflect his/her feelings.

c. Get back on the normal routine as soon as possible. Being in the normal routine provides a sense of stability.

Most importantly, remember that kids take their cues from the adults around them. If the adult(s) around them are calm and under control, the kids are likely to follow.

* reprinted with permission from Frank (2003). *The Handbook for Helping Kids with Anxiety and Stress.* Chapin, SC: YouthLight, Inc. www.youthlightbooks.com

Additional Resource:

The HANDBOOK for HELPING KIDS with ANXIETY and STRESS

A great resource for helping children deal with anxieties and stress is Tip Frank's book, *The Handbook For Helping Kids with Anxiety and Stress,* published by YouthLight, Inc. www.youthlightbooks.com (1-800-209-9774). The book provides a collection of practical, easy-to-follow tips and activities to help kids with various types of fears, anxieties, and phobias. The first section of the book includes insights, hints and suggestions for helping professionals and parents who are working to help kids learn to cope with their anxiety and stress. The second section is for kids themselves. It includes stories, activities, and suggestions that can help kids face fears such as:

- Sleeping Alone
- School Phobia
- Separating from Trusted Adults
- The Dark
- Germs/Sickness
- Monsters
- Bullies
- Being Overwhelmed
- Test Anxiety
- Terrorism

SELF-CONCEPT

The activities in this section focus on the development of a healthy self-concept. The activities offer the opportunity to acknowledge the child's strengths and positive qualities as well as strategies to manage the negative thoughts about our-selves. So much of our outlook on life is rooted in our own perception of our-selves and our abilities. A strong self-concept will allow us to acknowledge and appreciate our strengths and the things we can do well, and develop positive thoughts and skills to deal with life when things do not go "right."

Self-Concept

Activity: BUBBLE POWER

Purpose: To provide a playful way to talk about positive qualities

Materials: Bottle of bubbles with bubble wand

Procedure: Blow the bubbles in the air and tell the child to give an answer each time he / she pops the bubble. Present the following questions and allow the child to think of different answers before the bubbles are blown:

- Name things that you like to do.
- List some things you do well.
- Share good qualities about your self like - caring, honest, helpful, etc.
- Name some nice things you have said to your friends or done for them lately.

Activity: JEWEL FLOWER

Purpose: To appreciate our personal good qualities

Materials: Copy of the Jewel Flower Worksheet, plastic color jewels often found at dollar stores or department stores, glue / paste

Procedure: Encourage the child to share good qualities about his / herself. Propose positive qualities you know are true about the child. Have the child select the top 6 good qualities that best describes him / herself. Write these qualities on the petals of the "Jewel Flower Worksheet." Have the child select a jewel to glue / paste in the center of the flower. Correlate the jewel with the child being a real treasure – a valued jewel. Encourage the child to display his / her completed flower in a place he/she can continually be reminded of the good qualities.

JEWEL FLOWER WORKSHEET

Name: ______________________________

ERASEABLE OR PERMANENT MARKER

Purpose: To choose not to focus on our mistakes and hurtful statements from others but to focus instead on our good qualities and what we do well

Procedure: Talk about the use of dry erase marker / eraser and permanent marker. Point out how with the dry erase marker the information can be erased versus the permanent marker that remains. Explain that there are some things that happen – such as people teasing us, making a mistake, etc.- that we don't want to keep in our head and remember so we should "pretend" to write this in our head with a dry erase marker so we can soon erase it and forget it. On the other hand there are complimentary things that people say and good things we do that we want to remember and keep in our head therefore we should "pretend" to use our permanent marker to write these in our head so they stay with us. (Remember the emphasis with the marker is on "pretend.")

Ask for examples of different situations and decide which to use: the dry erase marker and eraser or permanent marker. Encourage them to carry around their "pretend" dry erase marker and eraser and "pretend" permanent marker for future situations.

Activity: WHAT WOULD THEY SAY?

Purpose: To gain insight from another caring person's perception of him / her

Materials: Copy of the "What Would They Say? Worksheet," pencil / pen

Procedure: Talk about how it helps to listen to nice things caring people in our life have to say about us. Review the worksheet taking "guesses" at what they might say. Then instruct the student to ask that adult and record their answers. Review in a follow-up session.

Worksheet:

WHAT WOULD THEY SAY?

WHAT IS SOMETHING NICE YOUR PARENTS WOULD SAY ABOUT YOU?

___

ASK THEM: WHAT DID THEY SAY?

___

___

WHAT IS SOMETHING NICE YOUR GRANDPARENTS WOULD SAY ABOUT YOU?

___

ASK THEM: WHAT DID THEY SAY?

___

___

WHAT IS SOMETHING NICE YOUR TEACHER WOULD SAY ABOUT YOU?

___

ASK THEM: WHAT DID THEY SAY?

___

___

WHAT IS SOMETHING NICE YOUR FRIEND WOULD SAY ABOUT YOU?

___

ASK THEM: WHAT DID THEY SAY?

___

___

Activity:

INSIDE BEAUTY - THE BUTTERFLY

Purpose: To focus on the importance of who we are versus how we look

Materials: *(Optional)* Caterpillar / butterfly changeable puppet

Procedure: Ask the student what they know about a caterpillar? Review how a caterpillar spins a cocoon and then emerges as a beautiful butterfly. Together create a story entitled: "The Caterpillar Alias: The Beautiful Butterfly." Use story sentences such as the following to provide a guideline for the student to create the story.

There once was a caterpillar named __________________. She looked like a regular caterpillar on the outside with a __________________ body and __________________.
One day she headed across the meadow to the pond where the forest creatures gathered. She liked to be at the pond except when some of the forest creatures would tease her. They would say, "______________________
____."
And "____." This made __________________ feel ____________. She crawled away with her head down. She knew she was a regular caterpillar on the outside but a terrific caterpillar on the inside – but they didn't seem to take the time to notice. She began to question the good things about her own self. She began to cry. The wise owl who had been sleeping nearby awoke when he heard her crying. He asked what was wrong and the caterpillar told him. The wise owl said,
"____." The caterpillar thanked the wise owl for his help. __________________ , the caterpillar, became tired so she made herself comfortable in the branch of a tree. She started to twist and turn and before you knew it she had spun a cocoon around herself. Feeling warm and comfortable she feel asleep. She had a good dream about herself - of the good things about her. She dreamed that she was ____
____. When she awoke she felt different. As she moved about, the cocoon fell from her body. In the light of day she realized that she was not only beautiful on the inside but now was beautiful on the outside for she had become a beautiful butterfly. She spread her wings and fluttered out into the world.

Discuss the story. Encourage the student to focus on the beauty on the inside – his / her good qualities and good character traits.

Activity:

INVISIBLE ARMOR

Purpose: To use his / her invisible armor to block negative statements from others and maintain a positive self-concept

Materials: *(Optional)* Poster paper, markers, foil, scissors

Procedure: Discuss the purpose in earlier years of an armor and shield – to protect against attacks by arrows and swords. Relate that today we don't have real arrows and swords coming at us but we may have the invisible arrows and swords when people pick on us or tease us. Point out how we can allow the picking and teasing to bother and hurt us or we can have our invisible armor up to block the picking and teasing. With our armors we can protect ourselves and our self-concept.

Create examples of teasing, then practice holding up the pretend invisible armor and review the positive thoughts we can think to strengthen the armor against teasing.

Optional: If the student would benefit from a visual and hands-on armor, have them create an armor. Cut out of poster paper the shape of an armor, add foil and decorate with strengths and positive thoughts.

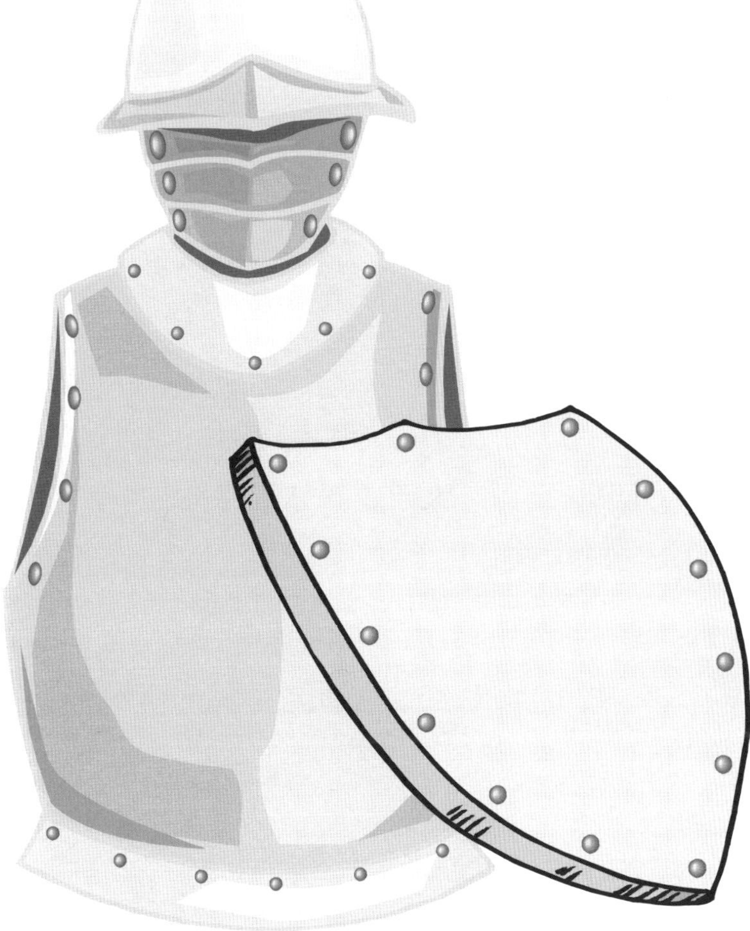

Activity: LIVING WITH MISTAKES

Purpose: To help students deal with their mistakes in a way that is healthy, positive, and appropriate

Materials: Puppet

Procedure: Ask the student the following questions:

What do you think the word "mistake" means?

- You may summarize a mistake as something that accidentally turned out wrong.

Does everybody make mistakes?

- Reassure the student that everyone makes mistakes and that no one is perfect.

What are some examples of mistakes we make?

- You may add examples such as: walking into the wrong classroom the first day of school, dropping or spilling something, bumping into someone, completing the wrong page for homework, or making a mistake while learning something new.

Explain to the Student:

Many of our mistakes can be categorized under the following areas. With the examples the student shared, decide which kind of mistake it was:

KINDS OF MISTAKES

- Mistake made from difficulty learning something new
- Mistake made when the person is not trying their best or thinking clearly
- Mistake made just because...accidents happen.

How might we feel when we make a mistake?

What do we sometimes do that doesn't help when we make a mistake?

- Encourage such answers as: get mad and quit, feel down on ourselves that we are not capable, try to cover the mistake up, or try to blame others.

What can we do to help when we make a mistake?

- Accept that it's normal and okay to make mistakes, learn from the mistake, keep trying, etc.

Introduce a puppet friend who feels just awful because of a mistake he made. Tell the student that your puppet friend needs some advice about how to "survive" the mistake and ask if he / she is willing to help the puppet. Proceed by creating a story about a mistake (perhaps similar to a mistake the student shared earlier) and ask what he / she could do. Use your counseling skills to continue creating the puppet's story by having the puppet share such questions as: "But I feel just awful, what should I do? say? or tell myself?" Compliment the student on their "good advice."

Friendship

The ability to make and keep friends is an important part of a child's development. The activities in the first part of this section deal with *friendship development*. It is important to know how to make friends - how to connect with others - and to know how and what to say to others.

The second part of this section provides activities for reviewing *friendly behaviors*. These activities provide an opportunity to review our own behaviors and assess if it is conducive to friendships.

The last part of this section addresses *friendship problems*. Problems will and do arise in getting along with others. These activities address strategies to handle conflict with others – including teasing and bullying.

Friendship

Activity: DESCRIBE A FRIEND

Purpose: To discuss qualities and characteristics of a friend

Materials: Bulletin board paper and markers

Procedure: Draw the outline of the child on the paper. Together create a friend on paper by determining the qualities and characteristics needed to be a good friend and writing these on the paper friend outline. Questions used to guide the discussion may be:

- **What does it mean to be a good friend?**
- **What would a good friend be saying and doing?**
- **What kind of look would a good friend have on their face?**
- **What kind of character traits would be important for a friend to have?**

Have the child compare his/her friendship traits with those discussed and written on the paper outline. Decide which friendship traits the child would like to develop to become a better friend and make a specific plan to include these new skills.

BODY TALK

Purpose: To be aware of what your body posture communicates

Materials: Mirror

Procedure: Ask the student to make the facial and body expressions for the following:

friendly face	shy	pouting
confident	excited	happy
sad	worried	unsure

Allow the student to review their expressions in the mirror and discuss what a friend may feel or think if you had that face on. Discuss if the body language helps or hurts getting along with others.

WHAT TO SAY TO MEET AND GREET

Purpose: To review and practice what to say when meeting others

Materials: 2 puppets

Procedure: Using the puppets role-play what you would say or do in the following scenes. Follow-up each role-play with a discussion of "what went well" and "what else could have been said."

Role-play scenes:

1. A friend going over to another friend's house to play.
2. At recess, you join a group of friends playing at the jungle gym slide.
3. Meeting friends at the bus stop.
4. Sitting down with someone at lunch.
5. Welcoming a friend to your birthday party.

FRIENDLY CONVERSATIONS CHECKLIST

Purpose: To learn and practice friendly conversation skills

Materials: Mirror, tape recorder

Procedure: Review the "Friendly Conversations Checklist" which lists the areas to focus on in talking with others. You may choose to ask the child to rate his / herself on each area of the checklist if you feel it would facilitate the process. If you choose to have the child rate his / her self use the score "3" for "Great," "2" for "Good," and "1" for "Okay."

FRIENDLY CONVERSATIONS CHECKLIST

- ☐ I have a warm, friendly smile.
- ☐ I have good eye contact.
- ☐ I listen and hear what the other person is saying.
- ☐ I make comments to show I am listening.
- ☐ I add additional information to the conversation.
- ☐ I make encouraging, positive responses.

Next allow time to practice friendly conversations. Conversation topics are listed below that you could choose. Before the conversation begins ask the child to use the mirror to "check" their facial expression to see if it is a warm smile, good eye contact, etc. With the student's permission, tape record the practice conversation. Then play back the conversation processing if there were any statements he / she could have added or changed. Compliment the student on what he/she did well.

CONVERSATION TOPICS:

- Ask them to share about a pet.
- Ask what movies they like.
- Ask if they like to play video games and what kind they enjoy.
- Ask about what they like to do on the weekends?

THE FRIENDSHIP PLAN

Purpose: To provide an outline to develop a plan to initiate a new friendship

Materials: Copy of the Friendship Plan

Procedure: Discuss the following plan completing the sheet. Role-play how to put the plan into action. Be sure to follow up with how the plan went and make adjustments if necessary.

______________________'s FRIENDSHIP PLAN

Name of someone I'd like to get to know better: ____________________

Things we may have in common that I need to check out – things we may both like to do: ____________________

____

____

What I will say to this person: ____________________

____

____

When: ____________________

Where: ____________________

If I don't "connect" with the person I will try again with someone else.
If it does work – great! I have a new friend.

IF... THEN...

Purpose: To help the student realize the effects of his / her behavior

Materials: Puppet

Procedure: Use the puppet to tell how someone else may feel or what someone else may think if you behaved in the following way:

1. IF you brag about yourself THEN...
2. IF you boss others around THEN...
3. IF you tattle on others THEN...
4. IF you are a sore loser when playing a game THEN...
5. IF you share well with others THEN...
6. IF you play well with others and include them THEN...
7. IF you give others compliments and say nice things to others THEN...
8. IF you smile at people THEN...

Ask them to evaluate their own behavior being proud of the positive behaviors and making a plan to work on and change the negative behaviors.

CHECK YOUR FRIENDSHIP BEHAVIOR

Purpose: To provide a rating scale to determine the student's friendship strengths and areas he / she needs to improve

Materials: Copy of the Check Your Friendship Behavior Worksheet

Procedure: Ask the student to complete the Friendship Rating Scale – encourage honesty. This scale can be completed by making a copy and asking the student to read and mark, or you may read the questions to the student and mark the answer he / she shares, or you may pick and choose only some of the rating scale items to read and mark (this is particularly recommended if it is a younger child). After the items have been scored then review the his / her answers, complimenting the student on his / her strengths and exploring what the student was thinking with the lower rating answers. From there create a plan of which items to begin working on for improvement. Be sure to add encouragement by complimenting the student for his / her honesty.

Worksheet:

CHECK YOUR FRIENDSHIP BEHAVIOR

FRIENDSHIP RATING SCALE

Name: ______________________________ **Date:** ______________

Directions: Mark the following friendly behaviors by rating the degree of which you show that behavior – circle either "4" for Great! "3" for Good, "2" for Okay, or "1" for Poor.

	GREAT	GOOD	OKAY	POOR
I compliment others.	4	3	2	1
I am polite and use good manners.	4	3	2	1
I listen well to others using good eye contact and head nods.	4	3	2	1
I smile at others and have a pleasant look.	4	3	2	1
I respect others. I don't tease or make fun of others.	4	3	2	1
I know how to meet and greet people.	4	3	2	1
I know how to handle friendship problems in a good way.	4	3	2	1
I share well and take turns.	4	3	2	1
I am willing to do or play some things my friend wants to do.	4	3	2	1
I care about how others feel.	4	3	2	1

Friendship behaviors I am proud of are ______________________________

____

____

Friendship behaviors I need to work on are ____________________________

____

____

FRIENDSHIP FORTUNE TELLER*

Purpose: To provide a creative format for discussing positive characteristics important in friendships

Materials: Copy of the Friendship Fortune Teller Cube on page 125 assembled – scissors, tape

Procedure: Roll the cube and name the word that appears on top. Discuss how that characteristic / trait is important in friendships. Share examples of a time or situation when that characteristic is needed in friendships.

*adapted with permission from Senn (2004). *Small Group Counseling for Children Grades K-2.* Chapin, SC: YouthLight, Inc. www.youthlightbooks.com

Handout:

FRIENDSHIP FORTUNE TELLER CUBE

Directions: To assemble, cut along the dotted lines and fold along the solid lines. Fold in the shape of a cube and tape or glue the edges together.

HONEST

POLITE

LOYAL

FAIR

FORGIVING

COOPERATIVE

Friendship

CONFLICT WHEEL

Purpose: To review appropriate strategies for dealing with conflicts

Materials: Copy of the Conflict Wheel sheets on pages 127 and 128, cut apart and assemble with a fastening brad

Procedure: Review the strategies for dealing with conflicts shown on the outside of the larger wheel – discussing and understanding how to use each. Next review the conflict problems on the inner circle. Discuss each problem, sharing thoughts and feelings about the problem. Then choose a problem on the inner wheel. Decide on an appropriate way to manage that problem and then line up the problem, the arrow, and the managing strategy. Continue to practice using these strategies for the different problems and add additional problems of your own.

CONFLICT WHEEL

Directions: Copy and cut out the two circles and the arrow on pages 127-128. Then assemble with the larger circle on the bottom, the smaller circle next, and the arrow on top. Insert a brad through the centers to hold the circles and arrow together.

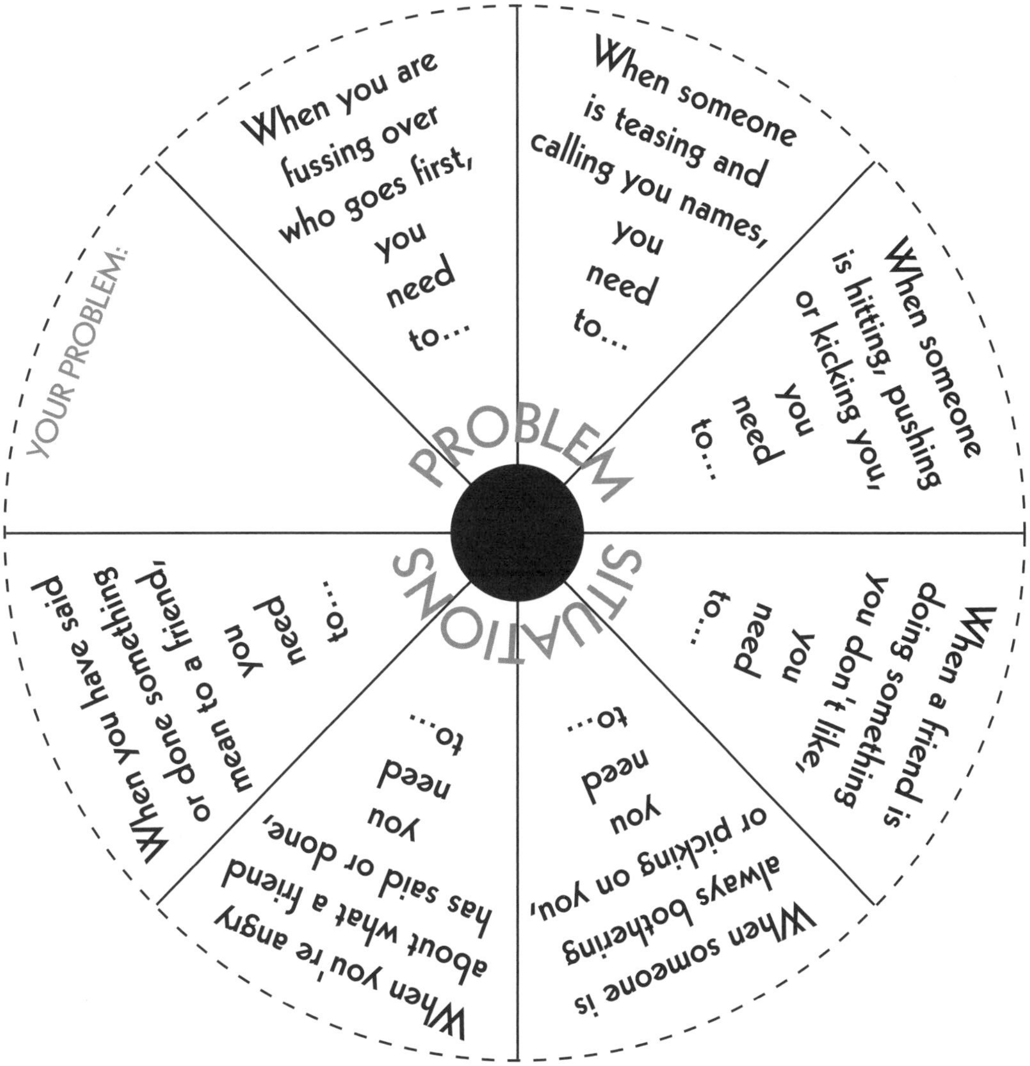

PROBLEM SITUATIONS

YOUR PROBLEM:

When you are fussing over who goes first, you need to...

When someone is teasing and calling you names, you need to...

When someone is hitting, pushing or kicking you, you need to...

When a friend is doing something you don't like, you need to...

When someone is always bothering or picking on you, you need to...

When you're angry about what a friend has said or done, you need to...

When you have said or done something mean to a friend, you need to...

Friendship

Handout:
CONFLICT WHEEL

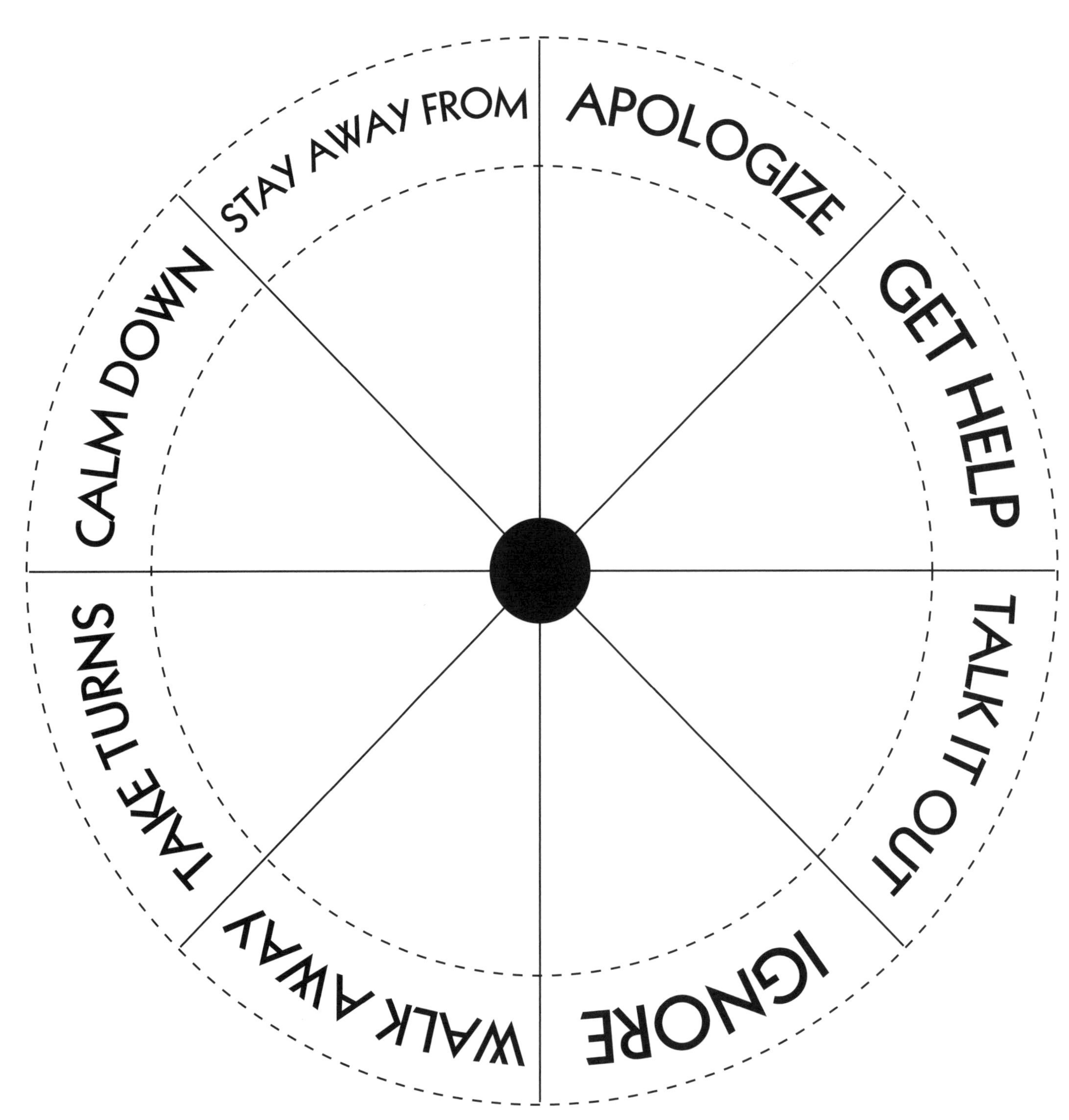

Activity:

TEASING / BULLYING... REASONS WHY

Purpose: To be aware of the various reasons why people tease others

Procedure: Brainstorm together all the possible reasons why people tease others. Your list may include:

1. Trying to "show off" and look powerful in front of their friends.
2. When the teaser is insecure they may tease others to make themselves feel more superior.
3. Some teasers have grown up being teased by others and they think this is what you are suppose to do.
4. Some people tease to get others to pay attention to them.
5. Some tease to get back at others for something they think they did.
6. Some students tease because they want to fit in and belong.

(Reasons...but not good reasons...)

Point out that typically when we are being teased we either think something is wrong with us or we think the other person is trying to be mean to us. Be aware of all the other possibilities. Explain that this may help diffuse some of the sad or angry feelings when we realize that their teasing could indicate a problem that the teaser may have.

TEASING WHEEL OF STRATEGIES

Purpose: To be aware of the various possible solutions to teasing

Materials: Copy of the teasing wheel on page 131, cut out and assembled with a fastening brad

Procedure: Turn the arrow to each solution of the Teasing Wheel of Strategies and discuss. Discuss when and how each solution may be helpful.

Handout:
TEASING WHEEL OF STRATEGIES

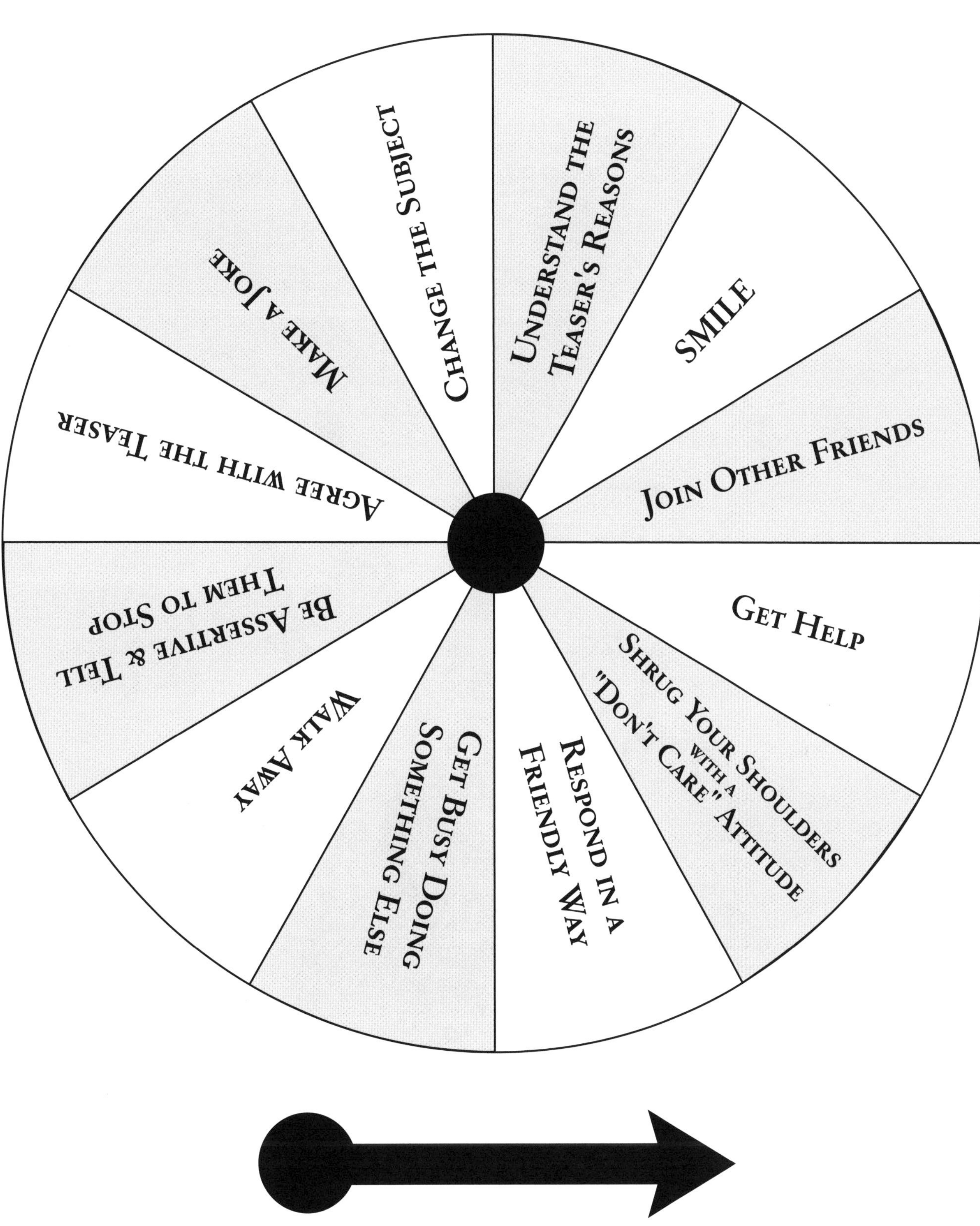

Friendship

TOUGH SKIN

Purpose: To provide a strategy to protect your feelings from being hurt by teasing

Procedure: Encourage the student to not allow the teasing to bother him/her – remind the student that what he/she is saying is not true. Share that teasing is no big deal unless YOU MAKE IT A BIG DEAL. To help the student not let the teasing "get to them" have the student pretend to put on a suit of tough skin over their body. Explain that with this tough skin on that it will prevent the teasing from "getting to them" and bothering them.

TEASING SOLUTIONS

Biblio-Counseling

Purpose: To share the story of Simon's Hook that includes five strategies for dealing with teasing

Materials: The book, *Simon's Hook A Story About Teasing and Put-downs*, written by K. Burnett

Procedure: The story, *Simon's Hook*, is a story about Simon who is being teased about his bad haircut. Grandma Rose helps Simon deal with the teasing through her fishing story. The fishing story relates fishing with the fish biting the bait to teasing with people reacting to being teased. The story gives five strategies to not react to teasing and gives good examples.

Read the story together reviewing the five ways to not react to teasing or not to bite the hook. Next, role-play the different strategies by using the hooks / teases given on the last page of the story. Compliment them on their good ability as the student handles it well and doesn't react to the teasing. Encourage the student to use these skills in real life.

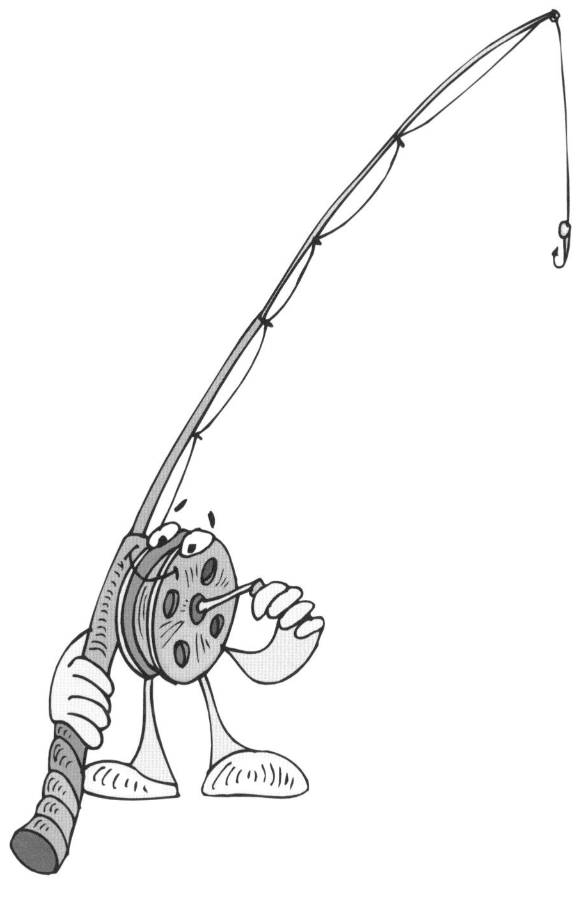

Activity: THE PLAN... TO HANDLE TEASING

Purpose: To provide a guideline or plan to follow to handle teasing

Materials: Copy of The Plan...To Handle Teasing

Procedure: Review and complete The Plan...To Handle Teasing. Allow time to role-play implementing the plan. Follow-up and discuss the results of the implemented plan.

THE PLAN... TO HANDLE TEASING

The problem is ______________________________

____

It usually happens when ______________________________

____

When it happens I first think ______________________________

____

When it happens I first feel ______________________________

____

After more thought I realize he / she may be teasing me because ______________________________

____

If the teasing happens again, my plan is to ______________________________

____

If that doesn't work then I will ______________________________

____

Good thoughts to help me deal with the teasing are ______________________________

____

Academic Support

Being successful in school and building a solid academic foundation is important to future success. The activities in this section address the academic success skills of listening, focusing, being organized, dealing with homework frustrations, knowing your learning strengths, maintaining a good attitude and creating a plan for success.

Activity: LISTENING SKILLS

Purpose: To share strategies to improve focusing and listening in class

Materials: Copy of the Listening Skills summary sheet

Procedure: Tell the student that you are going to "test" their listening ability. Explain that you will begin talking but at some point in mid sentence you will stop talking. At that point the student needs to share the last three words that he/she heard. Process with the student what they had to do to be able to "pass the test." Review the energy and focus that is necessary to tune-in and listen. Next review together the Listening Skills summary sheet given below.

Activity:

PACK IT UP!

Purpose: To review the student's organizational skills and target areas for improvement

Materials: A book bag that is stuffed with "junk" with no order - include crumpled papers, notebook with no labels or order to it, pencils in the bottom, toys, etc. make sure to include a math sheet that you will ask for later; a second book bag that is organized - include a 3 ring binder with index labels (labeled with a math section with a math paper in this section), books and pencils in a pencil zipper pouch

Procedure: Explain to the student that you have 2 book bags. Hand them, first, the unorganized book bag and ask the student to locate the math sheet. Then, ask them to find a pencil. Process with the student what they had to do in order to locate each item. Was it easy, difficult, frustrating?

Next, hand the student the organized book bag and ask the student to locate the math sheet and then a pencil. If needed guide them to open the notebook and read the labels. Again process with the student what he / she had to do to locate the items. Compare the experience. Include in the discussion the time it took to locate the items in each bag and the feeling (frustrated or calm) in locating the items. Focus on the benefit of having an organized book bag.

Ask the student to list on paper (leaving space between answers) areas that need to be organized to help the student be successful in school. List such areas as: book bag, desk, home study area, etc. Next, ask the student to name and write on the paper one thing he / she does well with organization in each area and one way he / she could improve. Encourage the student to use the sheet as a plan for improvement.

Activity: ATTITUDE AND SCHOOL SUCCESS

Purpose: To review attitude and its importance to school success

Procedure: Ask the student to explain what "your attitude" means. Discuss how the three words – Think, Feel, and Act – can define your attitude. Brainstorm different attitudes that students may have about school. Discuss how the following negative statements can negatively affect your schoolwork. Change the negative thoughts/statements to positive thoughts/statements:

1. I'll never use that subject so why should I study it?
2. This junk is too hard; I'll never learn it, so why try?
3. My teacher didn't explain it well.
4. The test was too hard.
5. I can't do it.
6. It got lost.
7. Mom forgot to sign it.
8. My teacher doesn't like me.
9. I'll just sit here until someone notices I'm not working.
10. I don't know what the word means, so I just won't do any of it.

Activity:

SCHEDULING CHARTS

Purpose: To assist the student in his / her organizational skills by promoting the use of scheduling charts

Materials: Copy of the Homework Assignment Chart, Monthly Scheduler, Long-Range Projects Schedule

Procedure: Offer any of the following schedules / charts if they have difficulty remembering the homework assignments or organizing their time for regular homework assignments or for long-range assignments.

WEEKLY	HOMEWORK ASSIGNMENTS				
Name				Date	
Subject	Monday	Tuesday	Wednesday	Thursday	Friday
Things to Take Home					
Things to Bring to School					
Messages					

MONTHLY SCHEDULER

Directions: Add the name and days of the month. Schedule your school day afternoons, setting aside time for homework and adding due dates of special assignments.

MONTH:

MONDAY	TUESDAY	WEDNESDAY	THURSDAY	FRIDAY

Academic Support

SCHEDULE FOR LONG-RANGE PROJECT

NAME ______________________ DATE ____________

MY LONG-RANGE PROJECT IS: ______________________

____

DUE DATE: ______________________

Directions: Divide the Long-Range Project / Assignment into smaller steps and list below. Assign a date to have each step completed. As you complete each smaller step, circle "yes" for completion.

	DATE TO BE COMPLETED	CIRCLE "YES" WHEN COMPLETED
STEP 1: ______________________		YES
STEP 2: ______________________		YES
STEP 3: ______________________		YES
STEP 4: ______________________		YES
STEP 5: ______________________		YES
PROJECT COMPLETED:		YES

Activity: HOMEWORK FRUSTRATIONS

Purpose: To review problem-solving strategies for managing homework frustrations.

Procedure: Ask the student if they have ever been frustrated with their homework before. Ask them to describe the situation, the thoughts, the feelings. Ask if he / she has ever been frustrated with homework and yet found a good way to deal with that frustration. Explain to the student that you need his / her problem-solving wisdom to deal with the following homework frustration situations:

- **When you are feeling overwhelmed with so much homework and projects due.**
- **When you think you can't do the work so why try.**
- **When you don't understand the assignment.**
- **When you feel that you are missing out on fun because of homework.**
- **When you start thinking homework is not important.**

Academic Support

Activity:

LEARNING STYLE

Purpose: To utilize learning strategies that best fit the student's learning style

Materials: Copy of the Learning Strategies for Learning Styles Worksheet

Procedure: Discuss with the student the three learning styles of the Visual Learner, Auditory Learner, and the Kinesthetic Learner. Help the student determine his / her learning style strength.

Together review the Learning Strategies for Learning Styles sheet and select learning strategies that would best help the student. Discuss "how, when, where" to incorporate these new strategies to help with the learning process.

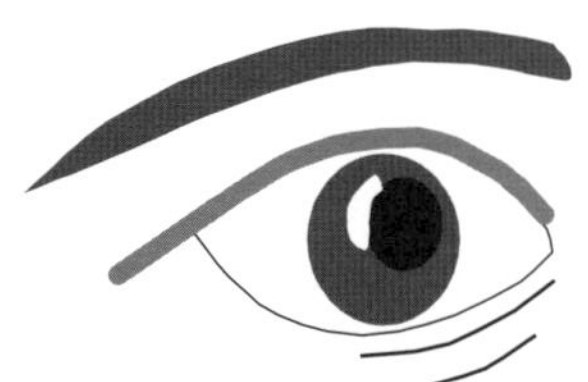
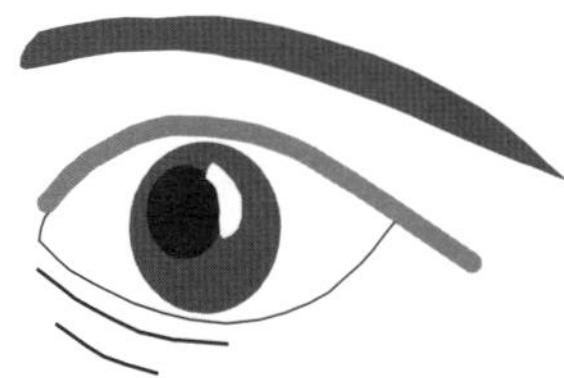

Visual Learner

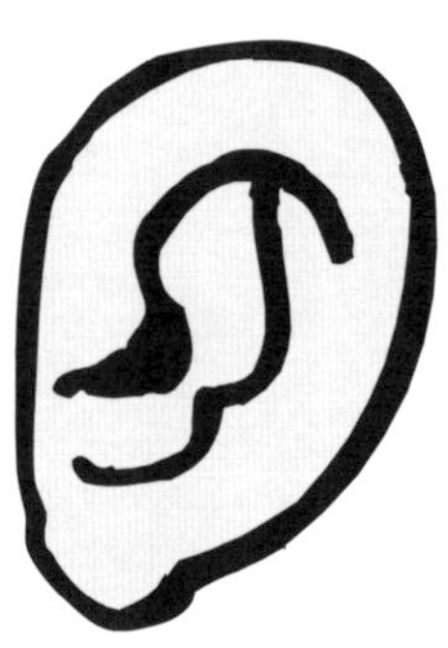

Auditory Learner

Kinesthetic Learner

Worksheet:

LEARNING STYLE

LEARNING STRATEGIES FOR LEARNING STYLES

IF MY LEARNING STRENGTH IS VISUAL LEARNER I COULD:

- Sit near the front of the class to see the board, etc.
- Take class notes to review later.
- Add pictures and charts to class notes to help remember information.
- Reread information.
- Create flash cards to help study.
- ______________________________

IF MY LEARNING STRENGTH IS AUDITORY LEARNER I COULD:

- Sit in the class where I can hear well and focus on what the teacher is saying.
- Read my notes, study guides, and / or textbooks out loud several times.
- Create a song, rhyme, or rap to help remember facts.
- Record important information on a tape recorder and play back later.
- ______________________________

IF MY LEARNING STRENGTH IS KINESTHETIC LEARNER I COULD:

- Use puppets or other characters to retell the important facts in studying information.
- Draw pictures, sing, or act out information to learn.
- Pretend to write the information in the air.
- Practice the information by writing it with sidewalk chalk, with finger paints, or shaving cream.
- ______________________________

Activity: COMBINATION TO ACADEMIC SUCCESS

Purpose: To provide a guideline to create an academic success plan

Materials: Treasure box locked with a combination lock, copy of the Combination to Academic Success Worksheet

Procedure: Ask the student to open the locked treasure box. Student's typical response is "I can't – it's locked – I don't know the combination." Ask them if they have ever opened a combination lock like this? Point out that each lock even though they may look the same on the outside, has a different combination of numbers to unlock the lock. Compare the combination lock and the treasure box - to finding the right combination to unlocking the student's academic success. Relate how each lock has a different combination just as each person has a different combination to unlocking his / her success.

Begin the process by pinpointing the area of academic need (gather information from teachers, parents, student, test scores, etc.). Next develop an individual plan for the student including their learning style strengths. Use the Combination to Academic Success sheet to outline the process. Discuss and complete the sheet.

To continue the analogy of the combination lock and combination to success, in follow-up sessions give the student a number in the combination lock each time progress is being made in their academic plan. Once all the numbers for the combination lock have been shared, allow the student to unlock the treasure box to find a reward, treat, or certificate in the box for their hard work.

Worksheet:

FINDING ______________________'s COMBINATION TO ACADEMIC SUCCESS

1. One specific academic area that I want to improve is: (short-term goal) ________

____

____

2. My learning style strength is: ________________________

3. Things I need to do to help me reach my goal are:

____

____

____

____

____

Any resources or materials needed for the above listed? ________________

____

4. People that can help me succeed are: (Describe how) ________________

____

5. I will check my progress: (when? and how?) ________________

____

6. My combination to academic success is:

__________ __________ __________

CONGRATULATIONS ON CREATING YOUR COMBINATION TO SUCCESS!

Behavior

The *Behavior Choice* part of this section includes activities to help the child review his / her behavior choices and the consequences, to review feelings and thoughts about the behavior, to discuss appropriate and inappropriate behavior and includes activities to compliment good behavior choices.

Behavior plans and charts are included in the *Behavior Plans* part of this section to monitor and provide a system to incorporate incentives for appropriate behavior.

The last part of this section, *Self-Control*, includes activities and strategies to help the child improve his / her behavior by strengthening the student's self-control and self-discipline.

Activity: CRYSTAL BALL

Purpose: To help the student use their "predictive powers" to guess the future consequences of his / her behavior thus helping the student make good behavior choices.

Materials: Clear inflated balloon placed on an upside down bowl to create the image of a crystal ball

Procedure: Ask the student what they know about a crystal ball. In the discussion bring out that we don't have powers to actually "see" into the future however we have very good predictive or guessing powers about what might happen. Ask the student to pretend to look into the crystal ball and see the future if the following was happening:

- **If you forget to do your homework – what would happen?**
- **If you talk out in class when the teacher is teaching – what would happen?**
- **If you talk back to your parents – what would happen?**
- **If you clean up your room without begin told – what would happen?**

Add specific situations that pertain to the child. Discuss with the child that by knowing what might happen, the consequences of our behavior, then we can use that to help us make good behavior choices. Encourage the student to STOP and LOOK INTO THE FUTURE.

RE-PLAY

Purpose: To provide opportunities for the student to practice strategies for correcting inappropriate behavior.

Materials: Copy and cut apart the Behavior Replay Cards

Procedure: Relate the concept of replay by discussing the use of replay in a football game – to replay in slow motion so you can see clearly what has happened. Point out that in life it would be nice to have a replay or rewind button at times to be able to go back in time to "fix" a mistake or behavior. Share that the next best thing is to rewind or replay it in our heads to learn what we could do differently if the situation arises again. Emphasize that it does not help to get discouraged by focusing on what we "should" have done but rather focus on what we "could" do next time. Use the following Behavior Replay Cards to get started and then add your own situations.

BEHAVIOR REPLAY CARD

You are daydreaming in class when you have been given a class work assignment to complete.

BEHAVIOR REPLAY CARD

You yell out the answer in class and your classmates stare at you.

BEHAVIOR REPLAY CARD

You make a mean face at your friend when you jump to the wrong conclusion thinking that your friend is talking bad about you to the person behind her when actually she is just asking to borrow a pencil.

BEHAVIOR REPLAY CARD

When your teacher asks you, you deny that you were talking during class.

BEHAVIOR REPLAY CARD

You let your anger get out of control when a classmate teases you about…

BEHAVIOR REPLAY CARD

You break in the front of the line to get out to recess.

PICTURE IT!

Purpose: Allows opportunity for the student to visualize or "picture" themselves with good behavior

Materials: *(Optional)* Paper, pencil, crayons

Procedure: Ask the student to close their eyes and picture in their mind their using good behavior... in the classroom. Ask:

- What does it look like?
- Feel like?
- What are you saying?
- What are you doing?

Ask the student to picture him / her self using good behavior in other areas such as in the lunch-room, recess grounds, with friends, at home, etc. Remember to process in detail their picture using the different senses.

Encourage and compliment the good behavior they created in their picture. Discuss how to make their picture a reality. As a reinforcer, consider allowing the student to draw their good behavior picture.

Activity:

WHAT TO DO?... ADVICE COLUMN

Purpose: To strengthen the student's ability to become solution focused in handling behavior problems

Materials: Newspaper with a copy of an appropriate "Dear Abby" type newspaper column, paper / pencil or computer or tape recorder

Procedure: Show the newspaper column as you discuss how problems come up all throughout life for people and that at times we may turn to others to hear their thoughts or advice. Explain that you need his/her help to give their advice and thoughts on some problems. Decide together if the student can best reply to the problem through paper and pencil writing it down, or using the word processor on the computer, or talking into a tape recorder. Create several problem situations that would be appropriate and helpful for the student to complete – perhaps let them choose which one from several choices. As the student works - compliment him / her on their focus, using their good thinking skills, reading their suggestions and guiding their answers if needed. Make sure to compliment on their creativity and good advice.

Option: You may choose the problem situations to be real problems that someone else is dealing with that may potentially be a good buddy for each other. If you go this route, make sure you get the individual's permission to connect the problem with that person, a willingness for the students to meet each other, and a commitment to help each other.

Activity: YOUR SUCCESS STORIES

Purpose: Activity that encourages the student to acknowledge and appreciate his / her successes.

Materials: Copy and fold to create the Success Stories booklet on pages 155-156 (To create booklet: cut along the dotted lines, place bottom half of sheet behind the top half and fold.)

Procedure: Talk with the student about how our life has both pleasant and unpleasant things that happen. Point out that we have a choice on what to focus on or think more about. Come to an agreement on the importance of acknowledging and appreciating what goes well – our successes. Enlist the student's willingness to complete the Success Stories booklet. The booklet can be completed together or the student may take and complete the booklet as a "homework" assignment.

Booklet:

When my parent told me to… I handled it well when I… **8**

I was proud of myself in class when… **1**

It went well when I was at my friend's house and I … **6**

I handled it well when the teacher corrected me, I… 

Behavior

Booklet:

Homework time was successful when I...

2

When the kid teased me I was successful in handling the problem when I ...

7

I handled a difficult situation with appropriate behavior when...

4

I had fun when my friend and I were at recess and I...

5

Activity: PAT ON THE BACK

Purpose: To teach the student to be proud of and compliment his / her successful behavior

Materials: Construction paper, pencil, and scissors

Procedure: As you and the student review his / her behavior choices, share with the student the importance of being proud when he/she does well. Ask the student to hold out his / her hand with the palm up and then move his/her hand to pat his / her back (shoulder area). While patting their back encourage the student to think about their good behavior choice and feel proud. Ask the student to trace their hand on construction paper and cut out the hand. Write the good behavior choice on the hand. Allow them to keep the hand and show to teacher / parent.

APPLAUSE BOX

Purpose: To practice choosing good behavior.

Materials: Shoebox, scissors, and a tape recorder with multiple applause / clapping / whistling sounds recorded. Place the recorder with the recorded applause tape inside the shoebox with a cutout space to press the "stop" and "play" buttons.

Procedure: Share with the student that you have an activity that will test him / her on how well he / she can make good behavior choices. Explain that you will read a situation with two behavior choices and he / she needs to choose the best choice that shows good behavior. Begin by reading each situation and allow the student to answer. If the answer is the correct good behavior choice then press the play button on the recorder for the child to receive the positive feedback for his / her good choice. If at first the student does not choose the correct answer, simply ask them to try again. Use your counseling skills to process with the student on how they knew the right answer, asking if the behavior choice would be hard or easy to follow through with in real life, etc. Don't forget to compliment the student's good thinking.

Good Behavior Quiz:

1. A friend tries to talk to you during a class lesson. What do you do?
    a. Talk to your friend.
    b. Stay focused on the lesson.
2. Your neighbor comes over and asks you to play but you have not finished your homework. What do you do?
    a. Tell your friend you can play later.
    b. Go play with your friend.
3. You have to miss 5 minutes of recess for playing in the bathroom. What do you do?
    a. Get mad and pout.
    b. Sit your 5 minutes and learn from your mistake.
4. Your teacher calls you down for talking in class. What do you do?
    a. You talk back to the teacher and deny that it was you.
    b. You apologize and sit quietly.
5. Someone is teasing you and calling you names. What do you do?
    a. Tell them to please stop, change the subject, walk away, or go get help.
    b. Get mad and call them names back.
6. Your teacher has assigned you class work to complete while he / she works with a small reading group. What do you do?
    a. Use your self-discipline in doing the right thing by completing your class work.
    b. You daydream and play around at your desk.

GAME OF GOOD BEHAVIOR

Purpose: To review good behavior in a fun, creative way.

Materials: Copy the Game of Good Behavior game board on the following pages. Cut an 18x12 inch piece of poster board and fit the copied game sheets onto the poster board and glue. Color with crayons or markers the game spaces indicated with the colors – blue, red, green, and yellow. You may want to laminate the game board for durability. Also copy on cardstock and cut apart the game cards. Need dice and game board moving pieces for each player – may use different color erasers, beans, coins, etc.

Procedure: Read the Game Board Directions for directions to playing the game. As the behavior cards are drawn and shared, allow time to discuss the behavior exploring the negative or positive consequences of that behavior. Ask such questions as:

- Why is that not an appropriate behavior?

- What might happen in real life if a student did that?

- How might you feel if you made that good behavior choice?

Blank cards are given for you to add behaviors that may be specific to the student you are working with.

Reproducible Game Cards:

You ask nicely to have a turn.
Good job.
Move ahead to the next blue space.

You broke in line.
Sorry, not a good behavior choice - you can't move ahead.

You began your class work as soon as assigned.
Move ahead to the next red space.

You raised your hand and waited patiently to be called on.
Move ahead to the next yellow space.

You kept your cool when someone teased you.
Move ahead to the next green space.

You listened respectfully when the teacher corrected you.
Move ahead to the next blue space.

When someone took your pencil without asking you, you politely asked for it back rather than getting mad.
Move ahead to the next red space.

Someone broke in line but you didn't make a big deal about it.
Move ahead to the next yellow space.

You were responsible and completed all of your homework without being reminded.
Move ahead to the next green space.

You used your good manners and said "thank you" when someone did something nice for you.
Move ahead to the next blue space.

You participated well in the class activity.
Move ahead to the next red space.

You didn't talk in class while the teacher was teaching.
Move ahead to the next yellow space.

When you sister teased you, you didn't get mad.
Move ahead to the next green space.

Even though you were in a hurry, you remembered the rule and walked in the hallway.
Move ahead to the next blue space.

Reproducible Game Cards:

You chose not to go along with your friends who were picking on others.
Move ahead to the next red space.

You used your self-control and didn't get mad when you didn't get your way.
Move ahead to the next yellow space.

You were polite and held the door open to help a friend.
Move ahead to the next green space.

You were playing with stuff at your desk rather than completing your class work.
Sorry, not a good behavior choice – you can't move ahead.

You were passing notes in class rather than listening to the lesson.
Sorry, not a good behavior choice – you can't move ahead.

You yelled at a classmate who borrowed something without asking.
Sorry, not a good behavior choice – you can't move ahead.

You were disrespectful when a teacher corrected you.
Sorry, not a good behavior choice – you can't move ahead.

You got angry when you lost recess for not following the class rules.
Sorry, not a good behavior choice – you can't move ahead.

You made up an excuse for not doing your homework.
Sorry, not a good behavior choice – you can't move ahead.

START

Draw a Card

YELLOW

Roll Again

Draw a Card

GREEN

Move Ahead 2 Spaces

RED

Draw a Card

YELLOW

BLUE

Draw a Card

Move Back 1 Space

Draw a Card

Roll Again

GREEN

RED

Move Ahead 2 Spaces

BLUE

Draw a Card

GREEN

BLUE

Draw a Card

YELLOW

Roll Again

RED

GREEN

Draw a Card

Move Back 1 Space

YELLOW

Roll Again

Game of Good Behavior

Game Directions: Players select a moving piece and place on the **START** space. Take turns rolling the dice and moving the spaces indicated. When a player lands on a **DRAW A CARD** space draw a card, read the card out loud (leader may need to do the reading) and follow the directions on the card. Allow time for discussion of the situation on the card. The first player to land in the **FINISH** zone is the game winner although all are winners if you choose good behavior.

Draw a Card
BLUE
Move Ahead 2 Spaces
RED
Draw a Card
YELLOW
GREEN
Draw a Card
Move Back 1 Space
RED
YELLOW
Roll Again
GREEN
BLUE
Draw a Card
YELLOW
RED
Move Ahead 2 Spaces
BLUE
Draw a Card
GREEN
Draw a Card
Move Back 1 Space
Roll Again
RED
BLUE
Draw a Card
YELLOW
GREEN
Draw a Card
Move Back 1 Space
Roll Again
Move Ahead 2 Spaces
RED
Draw a Card
BLUE
Draw a Card
GREEN
YELLOW
FINISH
Shine Like a Star With Your Good Behavior!

Activity: TARGET THE GOAL

Purpose: To target a specific behavior goal for the student and for the student to gain feedback in order to shape the behavior.

Materials: Copy of the Target the Goal sheet and if available a safe rubber tipped dart board game.

Procedure: Involve the student in an actual dart game if available. Process the steps needed to be successful – eyes focused on the target, throwing the dart and making adjustments in how to throw the dart based on assessing where the dart landed. If the dart lands outside the target goal you keep trying, when you land in the center target you feel proud and continue to work toward the center target again.

Relate the actual target game to the importance of targeting a specific behavior that needs to be improved – staying focused and practicing in order to achieve success. Show the Target the Goal sheet and explain how he / she can target a behavior goal to focus on. Each day or each class the teacher could mark, by circling, giving feedback about his / her behavior. Complete the sheet together, selecting and adding to the chart the targeted goal and then reviewing the possible scores and their meanings. (May need teacher / parent involvement to assist in selecting an appropriate behavior goal for the child.) Role-play and discuss ways to achieve the target behavior. Implement the chart. Check with the student at the end of each day / week to process the score and encourage him / her to continue to work on and stay focused on the goal.

Note: Need teacher's willingness to give the target feedback, therefore ask the student if they agree to involve the teacher asking for his/her help to mark the target. Consider parents' involvement in the goal chart based on the support they give, the child's view / thoughts about parents involved, and the benefit vs. drawbacks of their involvement.

(*Parents need to be able to focus on the positives of the chart rather than the negative. Most parents I have encountered have been very willing and supportive to focus and encourage the positive however there are a few I have encountered that have used the feedback charts to focus on the negative and on what their child is not doing as well. Use your good judgment.*)

Note: Behavior target goals need to be stated in positive terms such as:

- Begins class work as soon as assigned
- Participates by raising hand and waiting patiently to be called on
- Uses polite words and actions with others

NAME: ______________________ **DATE:** ____________

Directions: Circle the points earned.

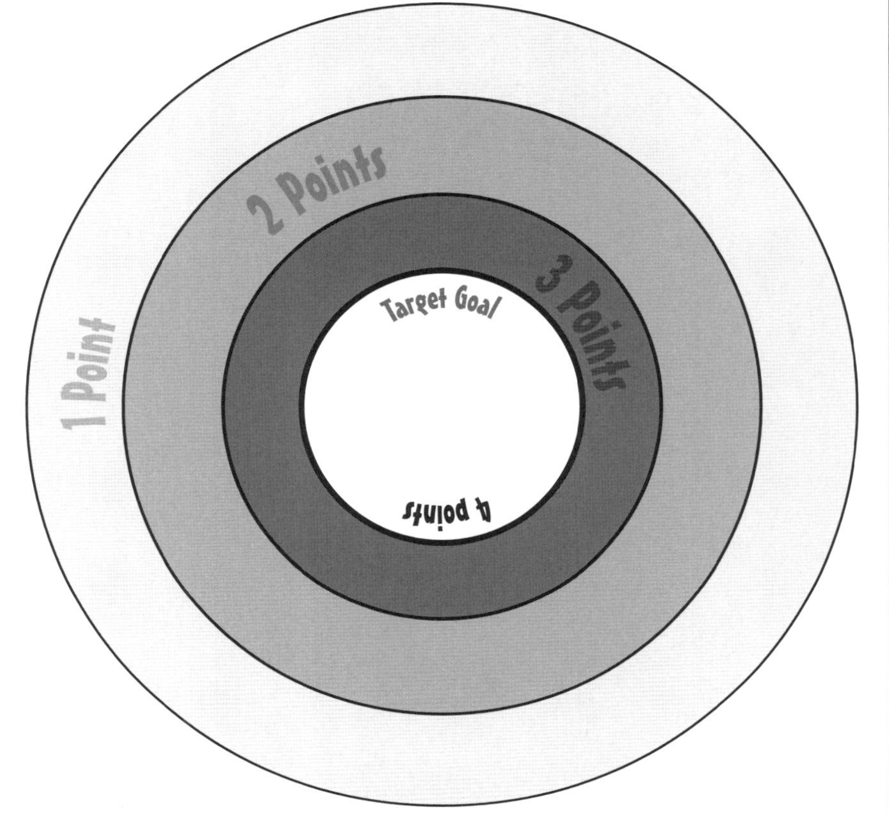

SCORING KEY

1 point: You're in the game – Keep working!
2 points: Good job, you're improving – Keep on working!
3 points: WOW!! Almost there – Keep going!
4 points: Excellent! You did it – You're a winner!!

NAME: ______________________ **DATE:** ____________

Directions: Circle the points earned.

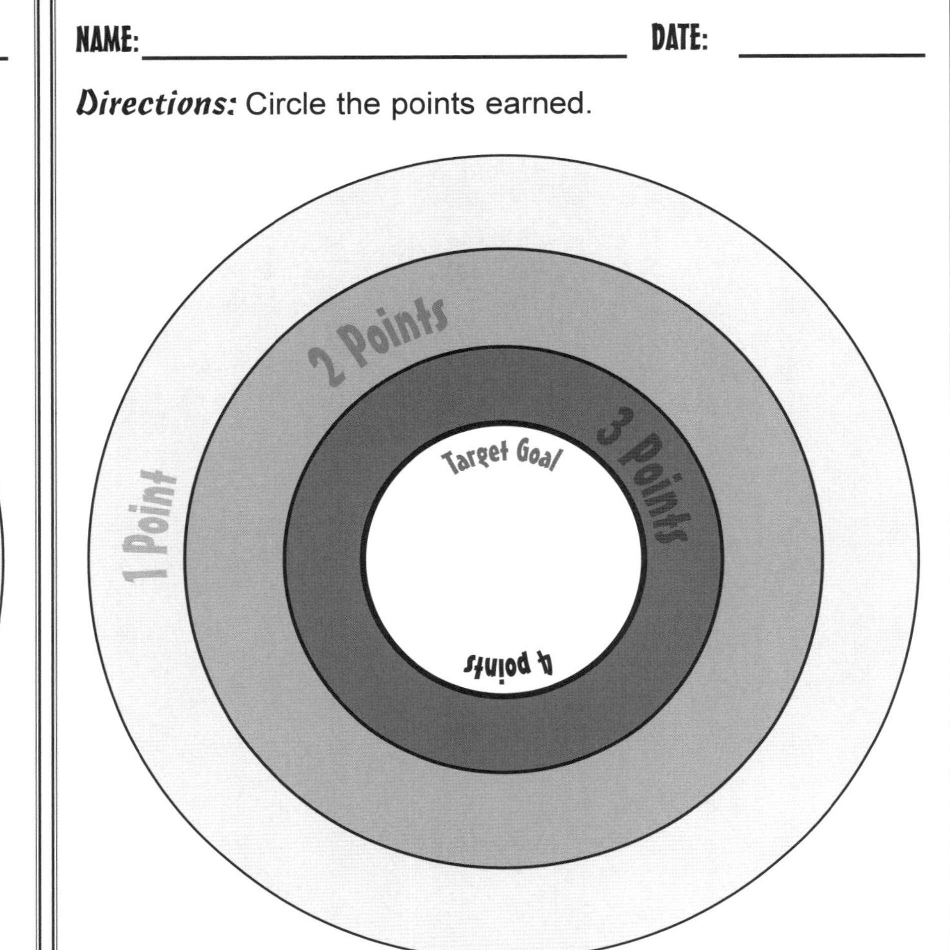

SCORING KEY

1 point: You're in the game – Keep working!
2 points: Good job, you're improving – Keep on working!
3 points: WOW!! Almost there – Keep going!
4 points: Excellent! You did it – You're a winner!!

BEHAVIOR CHARTS

Purpose: To gain a commitment from the student to select and focus on 2-3 behaviors

Materials: Copy of the behavior chart. Need a camera if you are choosing to take pictures rather than using words for the targeted behavior.

Procedure: Discuss with the student, gaining their willingness to select and focus on behaviors for success. Once the student has expressed an interest / agreement about using a behavior chart and has suggested targeted behavior then you need to talk to the teacher to gain an agreement to assist / mark the behavior chart and to review / suggest targeted behavior. (Don't forget to gain the student's agreement to discuss the student's behavior and chart with the teacher). It becomes a dual process to gather information from the teacher and from the student as to which behaviors to select and add to a behavior chart.

Review the behavior charts on the following pages as to which may work better for that student / teacher. Some like the open space to add a check mark or a smiley face / sticker when they have exhibited the desired behavior, no check mark or smiley face is given if the behavior was not shown. Some like circling a rating of 0-3 to indicate the degree of behavior and then adding points toward a reward. Possible rewards may be a homework pass, extra computer time, or a treat from a grab bag. Some students need feedback only once a day while others need feedback every hour – see the Daily Behavior Sheet. Review the weekly and daily behavior charts on the following pages to choose which may best fit the needs of the student.

Keep in mind the personality, cognitive level, and age of the child in developing an appropriate behavior chart. For the younger student choose only 1-2 behaviors to focus on. If the student is a non-reader it may help to take a picture of the child modeling each selected behavior. Then print and add their pictures to the chart helping the child understand the behavior he / she is working on.

Tread lightly in selecting rewards for good behavior. For some children just the positive mark is enough incentive. For others gaining points to redeem for class privileges works, while others may need the reward of a tangible selection from a treasure box. If extrinsic rewards are used to first shape a behavior make sure to pair the reward with the intrinsic reward asking them how they feel about their good behavior and reviewing the positive consequences of good behavior choices.

As you select behaviors to add to the behavior chart, write the behavior with positive terminology - such as:

- Begins class work as soon as assigned
- Completed homework assigned the previous day
- Raises hand and waits patiently to be called on
- Hands together and eyes looking at the teacher to listen well to instruction
- Cooperates well – follows instructions.
- Handles corrections respectfully.

When behaviors are selected, further discuss with the student what the appropriate behavior "looks like" and "sounds like." You may choose to role-play situations using the appropriate behavior and or list what you may say or how your body may look when exhibiting that behavior.

WEEKLY BEHAVIOR SHEET

STUDENT'S NAME ______________________ WEEK OF: ______________

LIST BEHAVIORS		MON	TUES	WED	THURS	FRI
1.	MORNING					
	AFTERNOON					
2.	MORNING					
	AFTERNOON					
3.	MORNING					
	AFTERNOON					
TOTAL:						

COMMENTS:

MONDAY ______________________

TUESDAY ______________________

WEDNESDAY ______________________

THURSDAY ______________________

FRIDAY ______________________

Behavior

WEEKLY BEHAVIOR SHEET

Circle the degree to whch the student exhibits the behavior:
3 = Excellent
2 = Good
1 = Okay
0 = No Score

Name: ______________________

Week of: ______________________

List Behaviors	Monday				Tuesday				Wednesday				Thursday				Friday			
Set Your Daily Point Goal																				
1.	3	2	1	0	3	2	1	0	3	2	1	0	3	2	1	0	3	2	1	0
2.	3	2	1	0	3	2	1	0	3	2	1	0	3	2	1	0	3	2	1	0
3.	3	2	1	0	3	2	1	0	3	2	1	0	3	2	1	0	3	2	1	0
Points Earned																				
Goal Met	YES		NO		YES		NO		YES		NO		YES		NO		YES		NO	

If you earn enough points to reach your daily goal, then you may choose a reward of:

______________ or ______________ or ______________

DAILY BEHAVIOR SHEET

DO YOUR BEST

EARN A SMILEY FACE FOR EACH BEHAVIOR FOR EACH TIME SLOT

NAME: ____________________

DATE: ____________________

LIST BEHAVIORS	8:00 - 9:00	9:00 - 10:00	10:00 - 11:00	11:00 - 12:00	12:00 - 1:00	1:00 - 2:00
1.						
2.						
3.						

GOAL: TO EARN ____________________ SMILEY FACES

TOTAL SMILEY FACES EARNED: ________

COST / TOKEN SYSTEM

Purpose: To provide a system of giving and taking items to help the student be aware of and manage his / her behavior.

Materials: Objects used to give and take to/from the student such as: play money, blocks, chips, straws, etc.

Procedure: Gain the student's and teacher's willingness to use the cost / token system. Focus on only one behavior in which you may give the student a set amount of coins, chips, etc. to begin the day (perhaps 5). As the day continues either take away or give to the student coins, chips, etc. depending on how the student is exhibiting the targeted behavior. The immediate feedback helps the student adjust his / her behavior. Provide either a praise reward for keeping / earning the coins, chips, etc. or provide an extrinsic reward for gaining a certain number.

The tangible / visible objects are helpful to remind students of the targeted behavior, however for some the objects can become a distraction. Choose whether the student will be able to keep the objects on their desk in a small plastic bag, cup, or box or do the objects need to be kept on the corner of the teacher's desk – out of reach but in sight for the child?

At times in using behavior charts and systems with selected students there may be other students in the class that ask, "Why do they get a chart and I don't… why do they get a prize?" It may help to answer: We all have times that different students need help to work on different things and this is to help __________. You can help by encouraging and complimenting when you see his / her successes. There will be a time when you need some extra help too one day. Thank you for caring.

SAY IT IN A NOTE

Purpose: To provide visuals or notes as a gentle reminder about behavior.

Materials: Prewritten notes with encouraging words and gentle reminders (*optional activity: Small sticky notes*)

Procedure: In consulting with the teacher regarding a student's inappropriate behavior you may suggest to the teacher the possibility of using pre-written notes to remind the student of inappropriate / appropriate behavior. This saves time and words as well as quietly communicates to the student (saving power struggles in front of peers).

To determine the statements to be written on the cards think of typical situations that come up with the targeted student that would be helpful to say to the student at that time. Write such statements as:

- Put what you are playing with away.
- Get busy with your work.
- Remember, no talking during class work time.

Develop a set of compliment cards such as:

- Good job! You're listening well.
- You started your work as soon as assigned – great job!!
- Your polite words were appreciated.

Type the notes and make multiple copies to hand to the student throughout the day. The teacher may also choose to include other students in the note giving.

Optional Activity: STICKY NOTE

For students who are constantly up out of their desk to sharpen pencils or talk or who excessively and unnecessarily go to the bathroom, etc. the teacher may choose to put 3 sticky blank notes on their desk that are used as passes. Each time the student needs to get out of their desk they have to turn in a pass. When their passes run out and if the student still feels that they need to be up then they need to "owe" 5 minutes at recess to make up for work missed for being out of their desk so much. This system is to help the student realize how much they may be out of their desk and for them to begin evaluating and prioritizing what is essential and what is not. Note: Use your good judgment to evaluate the purpose behind the student getting up so much. If there is a need due to ADHD disorder to be up and active or a medical need to go to the bathroom then do not use this system.

THE PLAN

Purpose: To develop a written plan to achieve a selected goal

Materials: Copy of The Plan Worksheet, pencil / pen

Procedure: The Plan sheet can structure the discussion to select a goal and then to make a plan of how, when, and where to achieve the goal. Complete the sheet giving encouragement and support for its success. Plan a follow-up to review the progress and regroup if needed.

Worksheet:

THE PLAN

Name: ______________________ Date: ______________________

My **GOAL** is to ______________________________

(a goal is something that you want to learn or improve)

Things I will do to reach my goal are:

1. ______________________________
2. ______________________________
3. ______________________________
4. ______________________________

People I can include to help me achieve my goal are:

WHO CAN HELP	HOW CAN THEY HELP
____________________	____________________
____________________	____________________
____________________	____________________

I know I have reached my goal when I can ______________________________

____

I want to reach my goal by the following date: ______________________

Behavior

Activity: SELF-MONITORING

Purpose: To provide a system for the student to monitor his / her selected behavior

Materials: Copy of the Self-Monitoring Behavior Charts on the following pages

Procedure: Self-monitoring sheets can be used for the student to mark and monitor their own behavior.

Chart 1: WEEKLY BEHAVIOR SELF-MONITORING SHEET is designed like a behavior chart in which you select 2-3 behaviors to monitor and then the student scores him/herself on that behavior. Examples of behaviors to monitor on this type chart can be: beginning class work as soon as assigned, raising hand to answer questions, or you may choose to focus on good attitude or body language of good eye contact, head up/shoulders up, pleasant look on face, pleasant sound in voice, etc.

The second, third, and fourth charts given are designed to mark the frequency of a behavior.

Chart 2: ROLLER COASTER BEHAVIOR monitors negative behaviors by first obtaining baseline information of the frequency of the negative behavior in order to set a goal to reduce that behavior. Examples of negative behaviors that you may select to monitor are: blurting out in class, out of your seat, or talking to classmates during instruction. After baseline information is obtained then a goal can be set to reduce the frequency.

Chart 3: 'BEE' YOUR BEST & Chart 4: SOARING WITH THE EAGLES provide a system of marking a positive behavior to continue encouraging and increasing. Examples of positive behaviors are: giving compliments to others, smiling, completing an assignment, participating in class discussions, etc.

Chart 5: INCENTIVE BRACELET that the student can cut out and tape around their wrist as a bracelet. Each time the student exhibits the selected behavior then they can color in one of the shapes. The selected behavior may be: completing a class assignment or participating in class by answering a question or adding to the discussion, or nice things or complimenting others.

Note: Self-monitoring scales are most effective when the student is enthusiastic and has the desire to improve their own behavior. With the structure and the support the counselor gives in reviewing/processing the scored charts it can result in student success. Remember though that self-monitoring charts are only effective if the student can accurately and honestly rate their behavior. During the process you may ask the student if it would be helpful to share with their teacher their completed ratings to see if the teacher would agree or disagree with the students rating. This may provide a more complete picture.

WEEKLY BEHAVIOR SELF-MONITORING SHEET

STUDENT'S NAME ______________________________ WEEK OF: ____________________

Directions: Choose 2-3 behaviors that you want to monitor to improve and write them in the numbered spaces below. At the end of the morning and again at the end of the school day, think and then mark how you did with that behavior. You may choose to use the words GREAT, GOOD, or OKAY or perhaps a smiley / straight face.

LIST BEHAVIORS		MON	TUES	WED	THURS	FRI
1.	MORNING					
	AFTERNOON					
2.	MORNING					
	AFTERNOON					
3.	MORNING					
	AFTERNOON					

Behavior

Chart 2:

ROLLER COASTER BEHAVIOR

Name: ______________________ Date: ______________

Mark a square each time you

____
(negative behavior)

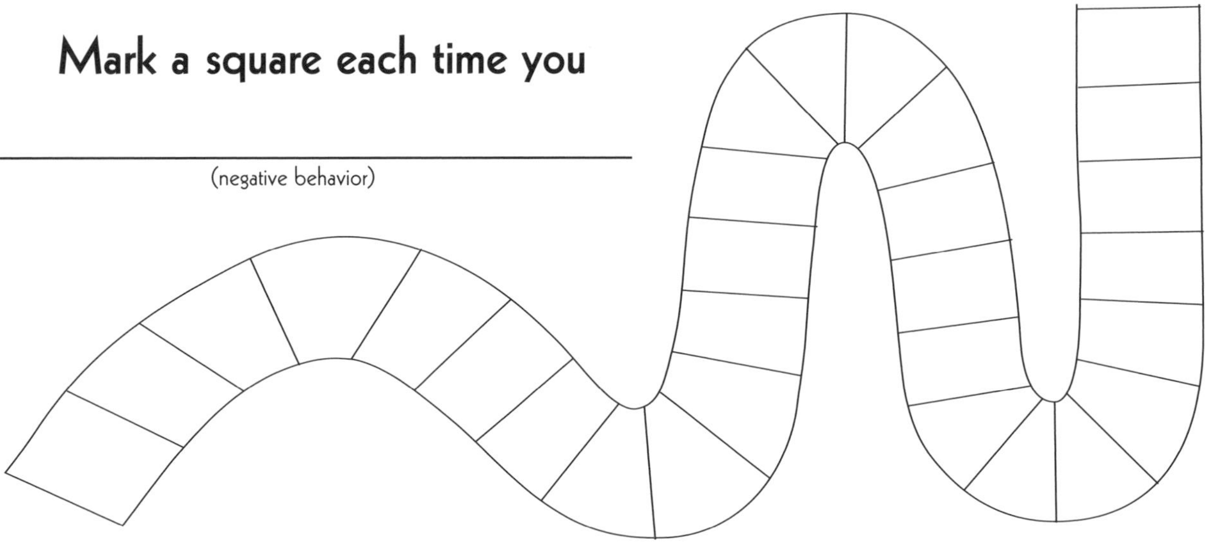

Next, set a goal to reduce that behavior. Work hard! You can do it!

Chart 3:

'Bee' Your Best!

Name: ______________________

Date: ______________________

Color in a space each time you show or do the targeted good behavior.

Chart 4:

Soaring with the Eagles!

Name: ______________________

Date: ______________________

Color in a space each time you show or do the targeted good behavior.

INCENTIVE BRACELETS

Directions: Choose a bracelet design to copy and cut out along the solid lines. Select the positive target behavior and add the information to the blank, "Each time I ______________ I will color in a ..." Add the name and date. Fold the bracelet along the dotted lines and tape around the wrist. During the day, as the targeted behavior is exhibited, color in a shape or jewel. Challenge yourself to complete as much as possible and to be proud of the good behavior.

Name: ______________________ Date: ______________

Each time I ______________________ I will color in a shape.

Name: ______________________ Date: ______________

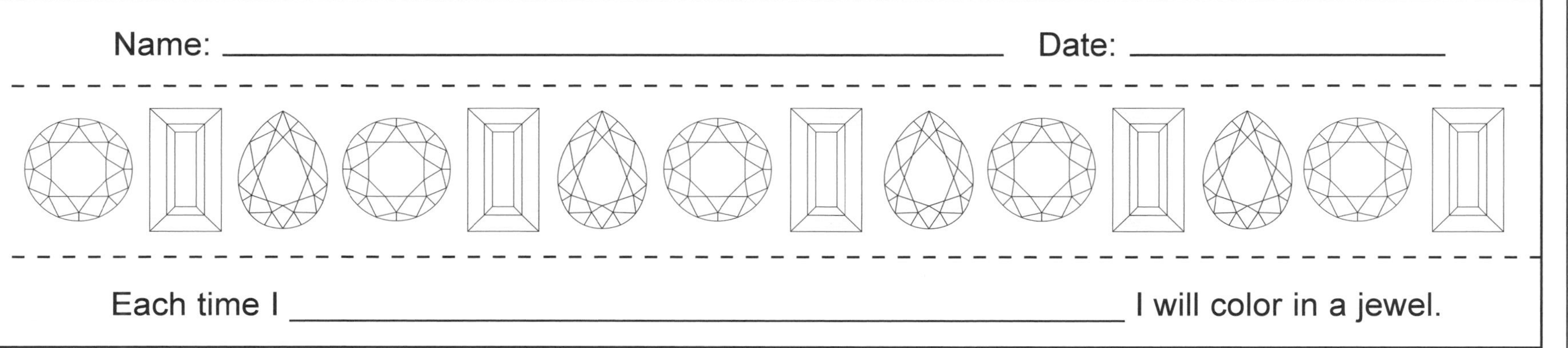

Each time I ______________________ I will color in a jewel.

BRAIN MESSAGE - B.R.T.

Purpose: To realize the key to self-control are the messages from your brain

Procedure: Present 2 phrases: Outer Control and Inner Control. Explain Outer Control as when someone on the outside needs to tell you to behave, to start doing something, or to stop doing something. Examples of Outer Control are: a teacher has to call you down for talking, a classmate reminds you to get out the right book, or a teacher has to remind you to walk quietly in the hall. Ask the student what he / she thinks Inner Control is. Arrive at the conclusion that inner control is when you tell yourself the right thing to do. Examples of Inner Control are: you tell yourself that you need to get busy with your work, you tell yourself that you need to walk quietly in line even though the adult is not next to you, or you tell yourself to remain calm even though someone is teasing you. Come to the conclusion that our goal is to develop and use Inner Control.

Ask where the message from Inner Control comes from. Elicit the answer: the brain. Introduce the concept of B.R.T. – Breathe, Relax, and Think. Stress the importance of taking a deep breath, relaxing, and thinking of the right thing to do.

Create situations to role-play using the B.R.T. method.

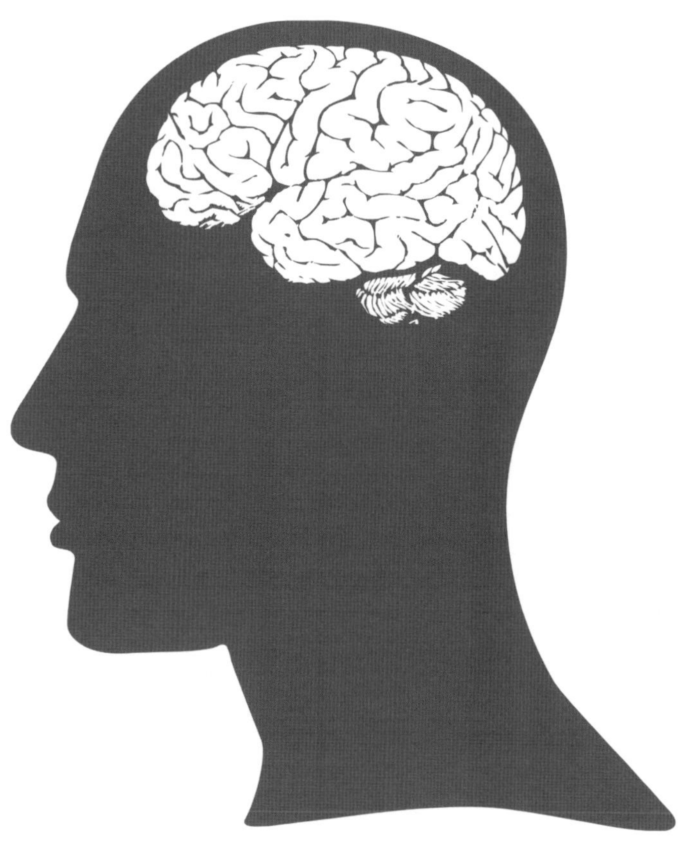

FREEZE

Purpose: Use of creative activity to practice self-control

Materials: Dice, copy of Freeze Activity Game Card

Procedure: Together define self-control. Ask for examples of when self-control is especially needed eliciting such answers as: when a person is being teased, when the teacher is giving instructions about an activity we may be excited about, etc.

Play the Freeze Game by asking the student to roll the dice and then begin doing the activity that the dice indicates on the game card. Explain that during the activity the counselor will say, "Freeze" and when the word is said they need to stop and freeze immediately. After the game has been played several times, discuss with the student using the following questions: What did you have to tell your brain in order to stop the activity? What did your brain have to tell the rest of your body? What did you have to do or say if you were having fun with the activity and didn't want to stop?

Relate the game to real life asking them to give examples of situations in which self-control (freezing) would be important.

FREEZE ACTIVITY GAME CARD

Hop up and down. 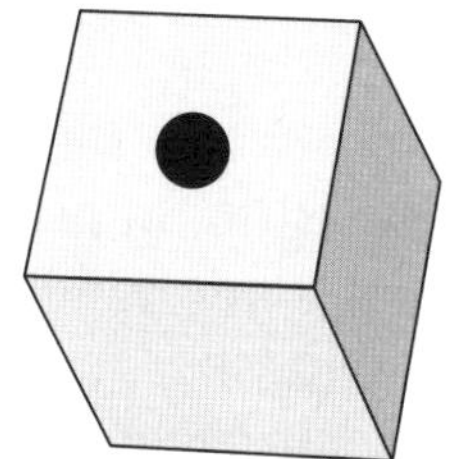	Do 15 jumping jacks. 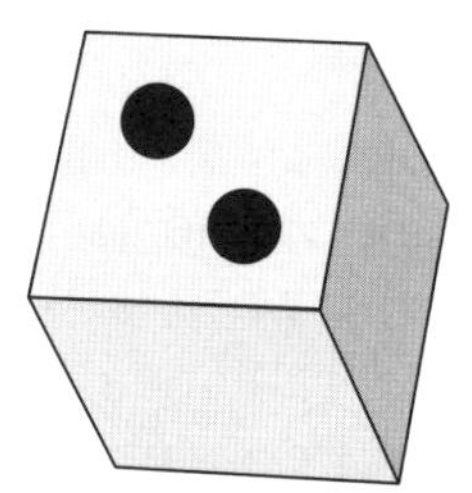
Count to 100 as fast as you can. 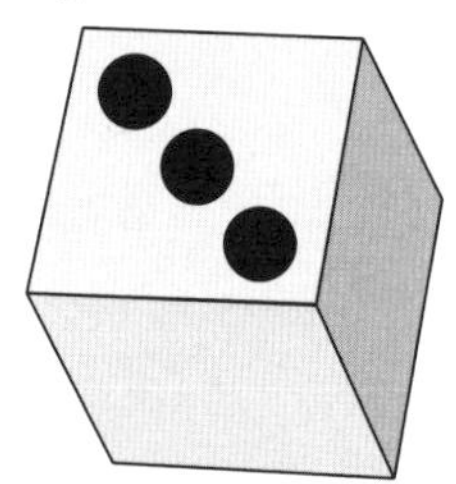	Do 10 toe touches. 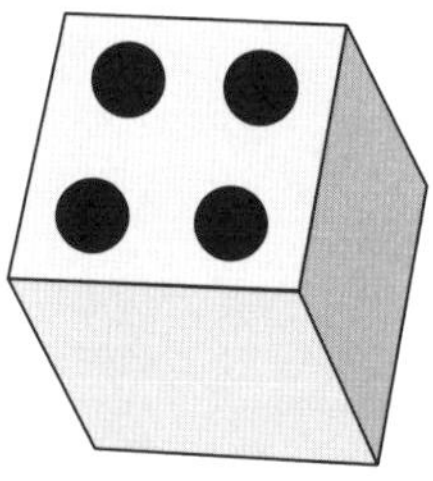
Sing the ABC song. 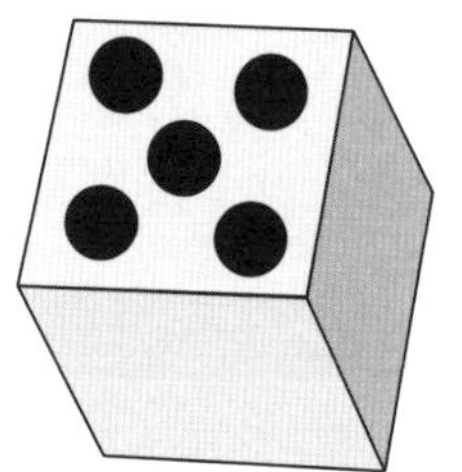	Dance around the room. 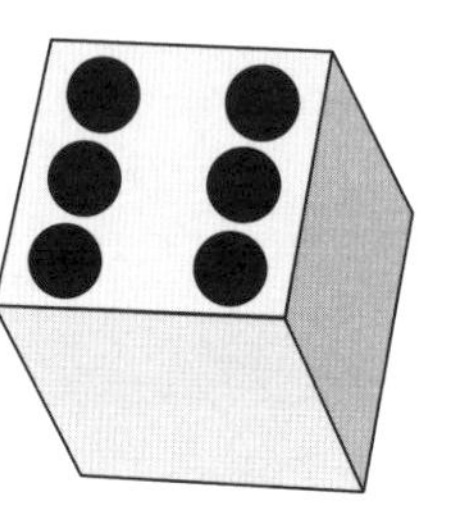

Activity: SOUND-PROOF BUBBLE HEAD PHONES

Purpose: To reduce distractibility

Materials: Your imagination

Procedure: Ask the student if he / she has ever been distracted by someone or something when trying to complete his / her work. Discuss how work takes longer to complete if we keep looking up and getting involved in other things. Stress the importance of using self-control not to get distracted. Present the following ideas to help the student resist distractions:

SOUND PROOF BUBBLE: Have the student pretend that a sound proof bubble surrounds him / her and locks in place when he / she needs to do seatwork. The sound proof bubble blocks out distraction noise.

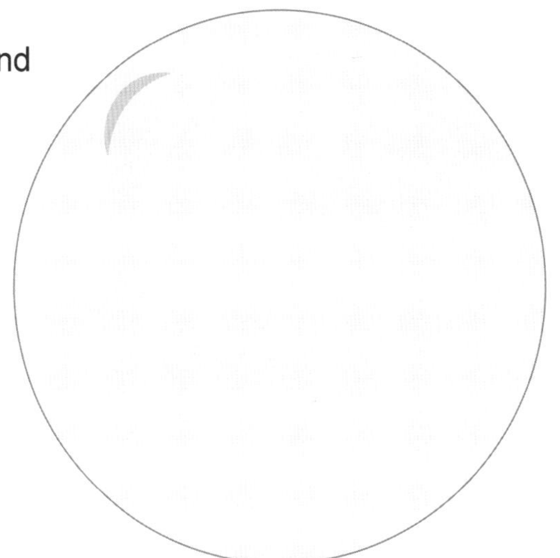

HEAD PHONE RADIO with THE TEACHER CHANNEL: Have the student pretend to put on a radio head phone set over their ears that is tuned to only one channel – the Teacher Channel. Encourage the student to use this when the teacher is teaching so the student can only tune-in to what the teacher is saying and cannot tune-in to a classmate trying to talk or whisper to him / her.

Activity: DE-MAGNETIZE

Purpose: To resist getting involved in inappropriate behaviors of others

Materials: Magnets, copy of the Ways to De-Magnetize Reminder Note

Procedure: Demonstrate how magnets can attract or repel. Relate this characteristic to people in that when someone is choosing inappropriate behavior we do not want to be pulled into it or be attracted to it but instead we need to turn around and repel or move away from the behavior. Discuss ways to repel or get away from the inappropriate behavior. Ask: What might you tell yourself so you don't get 'pulled into' the inappropriate behavior? Complete the magnet reminder note below. Encourage the student to take the note and tape to their desk or add to their folder as a reminder.

WAYS TO DE-MAGNETIZE

1.

2.

3.

4.

HUNTER AND HIS REMOTE CONTROL FOR THE BRAIN*

Purpose: Creative analogy relating a TV remote control to a remote control for the brain to help with self-control and good behavior choices

Materials: Lori Copeland's book, *Hunter and His Amazing Remote Control*

Procedure: From Lori Copeland's activity and storybook, pull the story to share with the student. Explain to the student that in the story Hunter discovered a remote control for the brain to help with behavior. Hand the student a blank remote control created from the remote control given in the book. As you read the story and share about each button, stop and allow the student to write in the name of the button on the remote control. By the end of the story, the student's remote control will be complete. Review with the student helping them learn and remember how to operate each button. Create situations asking the student to press the button that would help in that situation – allow them to explain. Encourage the student to take their remote control and use in real life situations to help them with their self-control in making good behavior choices.

Below is a brief summary and explanation from the story of each button on the remote control:

CHANNEL CHANGER – stay focused

PAUSE and FAST FORWARD – stop and think ahead to make good choices

REWIND – learn from your mistakes

SLOW MOTION – slow down, take a deep breath, and count to 10 slowly

COACH – for encouragement, to realize that it's okay to make mistakes, and to create a plan for doing better

ZAPPER – zap away negative thoughts about yourself

WAY TO GO! – be proud of your successes

*adapted with permission from Copeland (1998). *Hunter and His Amazing Remote Control*. Chapin, SC: YouthLight, Inc. www.youthlightbooks.com

Dealing with Divorce

Divorce means adjusting to both parents not being there all of the time, it may involve changing schools or neighborhoods, learning to share parents due to added responsibilities and other people, and perhaps adjusting to adding new family members. In addition children must also handle the normal developmental problems of coping with school issues, friends, activities, sports, etc. Changes in the child's family can affect their ability to focus and do their best in learning at school. School counseling during this transitional time is beneficial to be there to listen to the child, to help them realize they are not alone, to share with them typical thoughts and feelings that can be a part of divorce, and to strengthen their ability to manage and cope with the divorce. Only through helping them gain a healthy view of the changes can they get back to the business of learning.

Activities in this section provide questions, activities, worksheets, and journaling activities to allow the child to express their concerns and thoughts and to gain skills in managing the changes of the divorce. Also included in this section are *12 Tips for Parenting Through Divorce*. If we can assist the parent to maintain their own emotional health while encouraging them to continue to provide quality parenting during and after the divorce we strengthen the chances of the child successfully dealing with this change.

(See also the ACTIVITY: STAGES OF LOSS **in the *DEALING with DEATH* section. The grief process of separation / divorce often follows the stages in the grief process of death. Be there to listen to the child and help them move through each stage to the acceptance of the divorce.)**

Divorce

Activity: UNDERSTANDING THE SITUATION
INITIAL VISIT

Purpose: To gather information and the child's perspective on the family change

Procedure: The following questions may be used to facilitate the sharing and discussion process:

- How did you hear about your parent's separating / divorcing?
- How did you feel?
- What went through your mind about what was being said?
- Did you expect that this might happen or was it a total surprise?
- What questions do you still have about what's going on?
- Who could you go to and ask those questions?
- When things are bothering you which parent would you talk to for help?
- Can your parents talk with each other calmly together about how to handle this change or are there strong emotions involved?
- What have you found that helps you deal with this change?
- What else could you do?

Activity: YOU'RE NOT ALONE

Purpose: To help the child realize he / she is not alone in this process

Procedure: Offer to share general information about divorce using the frame of: "Would you like me to tell you some general concerns that other students' have shared with me about parent's separating / divorcing." **(Caution: this does not imply to break confidentiality of others and share specifics this is only sharing general information from your composite knowledge in working with students in this situation.)** Below is a list of general concerns that can be shared with the child:

- Who will take care of me? Will I have to decide which parent to live with?
- Was it my fault? If I hadn't misbehaved maybe they wouldn't have argued?
- I have so many mixed up feelings about the divorce, what do I do?
- I might miss the parent I'm not with, what do I do?
- How will I keep up with my stuff – going back and forth?
- I don't like it when they ask me to carry messages back and forth, what do I do?
- I don't like it when I come back from one parent and the other parent asks me lots of questions about what I did?
- My parents still fuss and argue, what do I do?

As information is shared ask if that is something that he / she has dealt with or can relate to. Use counseling skills such as reflecting feelings, asking open-ended questions, clarifying, and summarizing.

MY CHANGING FAMILY
BOOKLET

Purpose: To allow the child an opportunity to express their thoughts / feelings in booklet form

Materials: Copy pages 189-196 front and back to fold and create a sixteen page booklet. Provide a pencil, crayons, and markers.

Procedure: Provide the student with a copy of the "My Changing Family" booklet. You may choose to use each page as a discussion starter and then allow time for the student to write or draw pictures for each page. Or you may allow the child to quietly work first on part of the booklet and then share. Or you may simply use the booklet for discussion starters with the child not writing down information or the child may ask you to write down the information discussed.

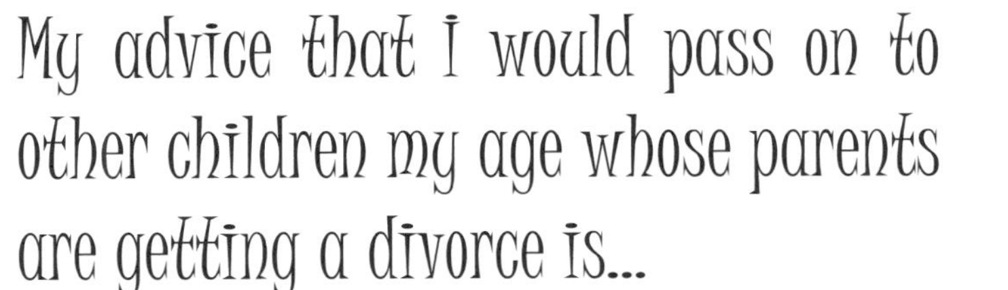
My advice that I would pass on to other children my age whose parents are getting a divorce is...

16

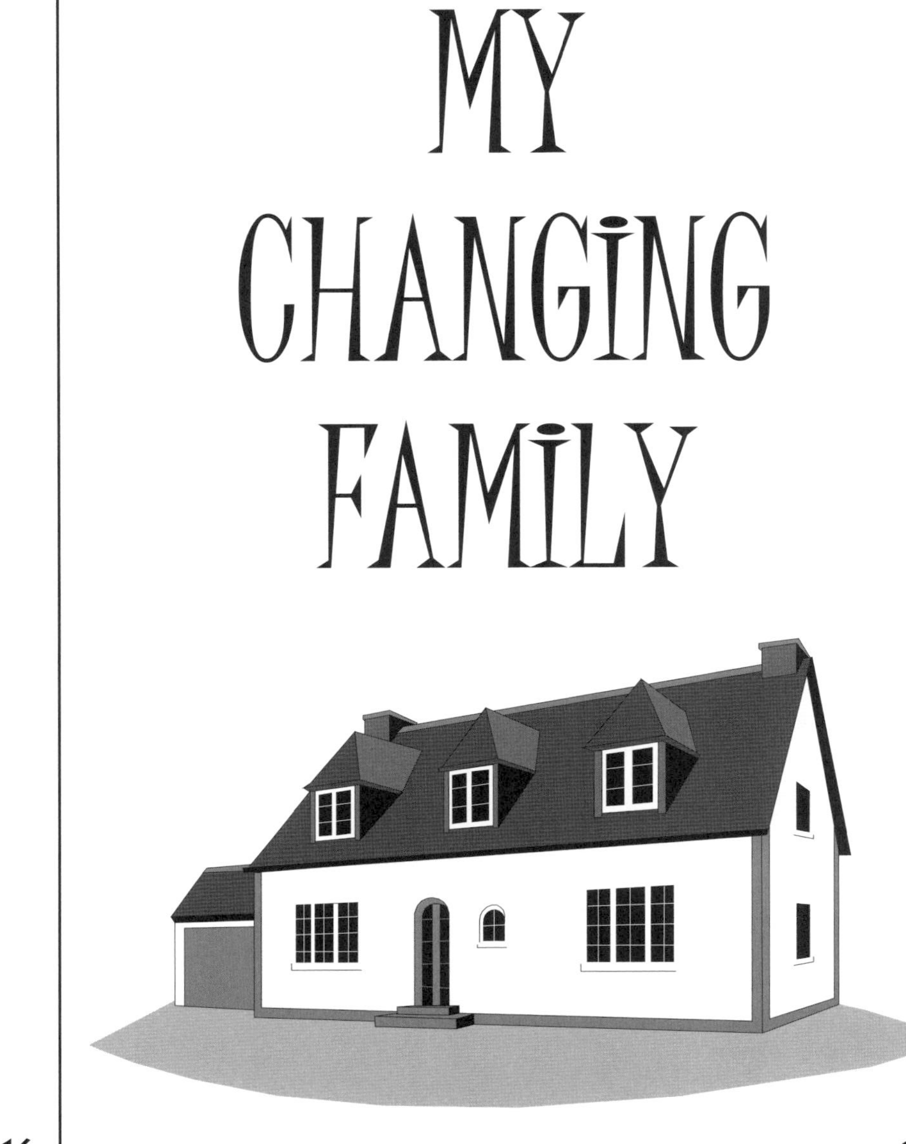
MY CHANGING FAMILY

1

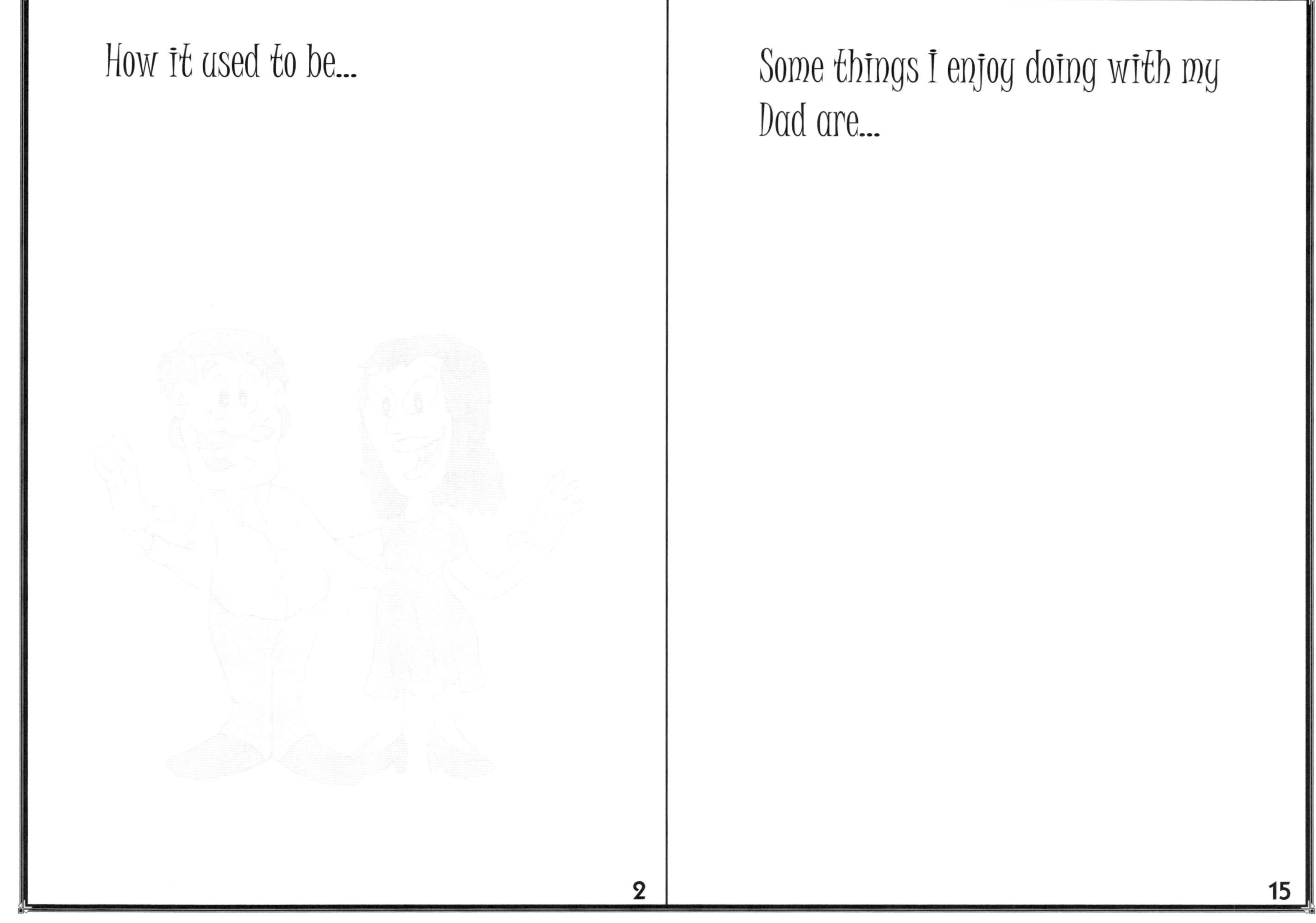

How it used to be...

2

Some things I enjoy doing with my Dad are...

15

Some things I enjoy doing with my Mom are...

14

How I found out...

3

The goodbyes...

Some things that I have learned to help me cope with my parents' divorce are...

1.

2.

3.

4.

5.

I've learned not to hold my feelings inside but to do something about them. Some things that I can do to help me feel better are...

12

What I miss the most...

5

What got better...

6

What really makes me mad is...

11

What I'm scared of...

10

Living in two homes...

7

How I usually feel now about my family...
8
What I wish is...
9

THINGS THAT BUG ME

Purpose: To provide an opportunity for the student to discuss things that "bug" them about their parent's separation / divorce.

Materials: Plastic bug, copy on cardstock and cut out the bugs on pages 197-199, place the cardstock bugs in a jar, *(optional) feeling faces*

Procedure: Hold up the plastic bug and ask if they have ever been bugged by a bug - perhaps at a picnic. Share how bugs can annoy and yet share how you can manage being okay even if the bugs are there. Set out the copied bugs that express things that can "bug" us about our parent's separation / divorce. Ask the student to pull a bug out of the jar and read together. Allow time to discuss asking if that is something the student can relate to. You may choose to include feeling faces to explore how you might feel if that were bugging you. Talk of ways to be okay and manage even if the bug is there.

Divorce

Handout:
I GET "BUGGED" WHEN...

Handout:
I GET "BUGGED" WHEN...

TORN HEART

Purpose: To acknowledge the "hurt" of divorce and to focus on strategies to repair the "hurt"

Materials: Clay, pencil / marker, red construction paper, and scissors

Procedure: Ask the student to take a ball of clay and shape into a heart, counselor can do the same. Then tear part of the heart as you ask if they have ever heard of the saying, "It's breaking my heart." Discuss / explain it's meaning. Discuss the "hurt" of divorce and then talk of ways to deal with the "hurt" and ways to feel better. As you review ways to deal with the hurt and feel better, begin mending the tear in the clay heart.

Help the student cut out a large heart from the red construction paper. Ask them to write at the top, "Ways I can feel better…" Allow time for the student to write or draw pictures of helpful ways to repair the "hurt."

Activity: THINK, SAY, OR DO*

Purpose: To encourage the student to find helpful ways to think, say, or do about concerns of the divorce

Materials: Tape, crayons and a copy of the Think, Say, Do Cube on page 202

Procedure: Together assemble the Think, Say, Do Cube following the directions and creating the cube. Explain to the student that when problems arise it may be helpful to think about the problem in a different way to feel better, or there may be something he / she needs to say to feel better or something he / she needs to do to handle the problem well. Remind the student that he / she does not have control of "what" mom or dad do but the student has control over "how" he / she will handle what mom and dad do. As the student shares concerns or problems about the family change with the separation/divorce, roll the Think, Say, Do Cube and use the word rolled to help guide the discussion as to how to handle the situation well.

*adapted with permission from Senn (2004). *Small Group Counseling for Children Grades K-2.* Chapin, SC: YouthLight, Inc. www.youthlightbooks.com

Divorce

THINK, SAY, DO CUBE

Directions: Copy the Think, Say, or Do Cube. To assemble, cut along the dotted lines and fold along the solid lines. Fold in the shape of a cube and tape or glue the edges together.

THINK THINK
THINK THINK

SAY SAY
SAY SAY

DO DO
DO DO

THINK THINK
THINK THINK

DO DO
DO DO

SAY SAY
SAY SAY

Activity: KALEIDOSCOPE

Purpose: To help the child see the good, the "beauty," in the family change

Materials: Kaleidoscope (inexpensive cardboard kaleidoscopes may be found at dollar stores or party goods store)

Procedure: Allow the child to look into a kaleidoscope. Point out the colorful stones and the beauty in the picture he / she is seeing. Tell him / her to shake up the kaleidoscope and look again. Ask if the picture has changed. Ask if they can see the beauty in the new picture. Relate the student's family change to the kaleidoscope by sharing that there was beauty in the family at one point when they where all together, things were shaken up with the parents separation / divorce, but you can look again and see the new "beauty" in the change. Encourage the student to look for and share the "beauty", the good things, in the new change. If you have extra kaleidoscopes you may choose to let the student take one with them as a reminder to look for the "beauty" in the new change.

Activity:

12 TIPS FOR PARENTING THROUGH DIVORCE

Purpose: To provide information / suggestions for the parent to consider that may help the child adjust to the separation / divorce

Materials: Copy of the 12 Tips for Parenting Through Divorce Handout

Procedure: You can provide this as a handout when parents contact you with a concern and / or share with parents of a child that you are counseling about their parent's separation or divorce.

12 TIPS FOR PARENTING THROUGH DIVORCE

1. Take time to reassure your children that they are not to blame for the divorce. Children often feel that it is their fault. They think that if they had behaved better then perhaps mom and dad would not have argued and divorced.

2. Be aware of the different feelings children facing a divorce often have. They may feel: sad, angry, guilty, afraid of the unknown, scared, or worried. It is normal and natural to have many different feelings about the separation / divorce and the changes. Help the child find appropriate ways to deal with these emotions.

3. Allow time for your child to talk about the separation / divorce and to ask questions. Explain the divorce to your children at least every six months. One explanation is not enough. With time, their ability to under stand what you tell them will change, and they'll have new questions and concerns.

4. Remember that a child cannot take the place of the 'missing' parent. Do not expect the child to turn into a grownup overnight and don't treat them like a grownup – sharing grownup information. They are children and need to be allowed to play and be a child.

5. Resist the temptation to confide in your child. Don't expose your child to adult information such as intimate relationship details or financial concerns. You will need to talk about what's happening, so find adult confidants that you trust.

6. Don't allow your guilt to interfere with parental responsibility. Try not to be overprotective or overindulgent with privileges or using material things to compensate. It's important to set limits and provide structure. At such an unsettled time, consistency is especially important.

7. Discourage your child from taking sides. Refrain from making unkind remarks about your ex-spouse where they can hear you. Children usually take after both parents. So they may interpret a criticism of one of their parents as a criticism of them.

8. Don't use visitation or child support as bargaining tools with the other parent.

9. Don't make your child feel guilty about enjoying him / herself with the other parent.

10. Respect the privacy of your child's relationship with the other parent. Do your best not to ask too many questions when they return from a visit. Allow them privacy for phone conversations. And don't use the child to carry messages, letters, or checks to the other parent.

11. Try to help your child maintain a relationship with relatives on both sides.

12. Establish new traditions for holiday celebrations. More than any other times, holidays and birthdays remind kids that things will never be the same. Try doing something entirely different to celebrate the holiday. Choose something you enjoy too – the happier you are, the more likely that your child will be happy.

Remember...time heals...

Dealing with Death

Dealing with death finds its way into the lives of all of us. There is no one "normal way" to react to death. Each person will respond in his/her own way, however there are phases or stages of grief. The activities in this section are designed to help the student successfully go through the different stages reaching the final stage of acceptance.

Activity: STAGES OF GRIEF

Purpose: To be aware of the different stages/phases of the grieving process in order to best connect with the child

Procedure: The "stages of grief," as first described by Elizabeth Kubler-Ross, that many people experience are: denial, anger, bargaining, depression, and acceptance. Grieving is a process that takes time and support to move in and out of the stages to the healing and acceptance stage. In talking with the student who is dealing with a death, you may choose to share with the student what you know about how others may think and feel when dealing with death. The information can be summarized as:

1. At first people may be in shock or deny that the person has died. In first hearing about the death it may be hard to believe that it really happened and that they are really gone.

2. The next three stages deal with confusion and painful feelings such as anger – feeling mad that the person died, perhaps feeling guilty of something you said or did or didn't say or do, bargaining or wishing that things would be back the way they were and sadness about the loss and missing the person.

3. The final healing stage is accepting what has happened – knowing that the person would want you to move on with your life and live.

Share information with the student about the stages, asking questions about their thoughts and feelings and using your counseling skills of reflecting feelings and summarizing.

Activity: GATHER INFORMATION

Purpose: To help the child talk about and deal with the death

Procedure: Adults talk and retell to help themselves heal. Allow the child to talk, play / replay, draw, write, etc. in order to heal. Ask questions, give support, redirect, and summarize their information. Encourage the student to express his / her thoughts and feelings and encourage him / her to ask for what they need. Be aware of the cognitive level of the child and the student's ability to understand that death is final.

Possible questions to facilitate the counseling process are:

- How did you hear about the death?
- What went through your mind when you first heard?
- Had the person been ill or was this an unexpected death at this time?
- Have you ever had anyone close to you die before?
- What do you believe happens to a person when they die? (reinforce the positives of what they share)
- Why do we cry when someone dies? (Point out that crying is more for ourselves because we will miss them – we know they are okay and in a good place. Share that it helps to remember the good things about that person so they can live in our heart.)
- Have you ever been to a funeral before? (Visitation and the funeral is a time for friends and family to get together and share good memories of the person and to say "goodbye")
- What is something special you will remember about the person? Perhaps something special you did together, or perhaps something he / she shared with you or taught you? You can follow up with this by offering to work together to create a memory box or memory booklet as a keepsake (see the following activities in this section).

Activity: MEMORY BOX

Purpose: To provide an opportunity to share and retell special memories while creating a keepsake

Materials: Box and special memory items brought in by the student

Procedure: Allow the student to bring in items of special memories to create a "Memory Box" of the person who has died. Items may include pictures, a special book that the two shared, items from hobbies that were shared, etc. As items are brought in encourage the student to share. Remember to use good counseling responses of reflective listening, asking questions, summarizing, complimenting, etc.

If the student is unable to bring in the actual items you can discuss what items the student may choose to put in a "Memory Box" at home. Listening while the child talks and shares about the items is important.

MEMORY BOOKLET

Purpose: To provide an avenue for the child to share about the special person who has died

Materials: Copy of the booklet "Remembering..." pages 212-222, crayons / pencils

Procedure: You can choose to use the memory booklet in its entirety or you may choose to pull certain pages to use in working with the child. Use your counseling skills as information on each page is shared and discussed.

REMEMBERING...

My name is ____________________

And I am __________ *years old.*

THIS IS MY SPECIAL MEMORY BOOK ABOUT MY

____

who died on ____________________.

Here is a picture of my special person:

Even when someone you love dies, you don't lose the person completely – you still have your memories. That person can always be a part of you.

MY SPECIAL PERSON DIED OF...

When someone you love dies, you feel sad. Even if the person was sick for a long time, there is no way to prepare for the feeling of shock you have when you learn about the death.

WHEN BEING TOLD ABOUT THE DEATH,

I REMEMBER...

I was told by...

The person said...

What I first thought...

What I first did...

Family and friends of the person who has died usually have a funeral or ceremony to honor and remember the good things about the person they loved.

WHAT I REMEMBER MOST ABOUT THE FUNERAL IS…

You probably have lots of strange and confused feelings about the death of your special person. At times you may feel like crying. It is always all right to cry. When you hurt inside it is important to let the pain out – and sometimes tears can help do this.

I FEEL SAD ABOUT…

HERE IS MY LIST OF THINGS I CAN DO WHEN I'M FEELING SAD OR LONELY:

Talking about the sadness takes some of the pain away. Getting busy with day to day things helps too.

Sometimes instead of feeling sad we may feel mad or angry. "How could they die and do that to us?" we ask. It is just as important to get the angry feelings out as the tears.

I FEEL ANGRY ABOUT...

WHEN I AM ANGRY OR MAD I...

Some people yell and scream into a pillow to get out the angry feelings, others play hard and get their mind on other things. Some write about or talk about what they are angry about. There are many different ways to express your anger, but it's important to remember when expressing your anger never hurt yourself or anyone else.

Feeling scared or worried about being left alone are common feelings that children experience. "If Daddy could get so sick and die, then so can Mother." It is normal to worry about the other people in our lives, but chances are they will stay healthy and be around to love and care for us for a long time.

I WORRY ABOUT...

A PERSON I TRUST THAT I CAN TALK TO IS...

SEVERAL THINGS ABOUT MY LIFE HAVE CHANGED SINCE THE DEATH SUCH AS...

WITH ALL OF THE CHANGES AND MY DIFFERENT FEELINGS I AM COMFORTED AND FEEL BETTER WHEN...

Sometimes it helps to write a goodbye letter to the person who died. It helps to get your feelings out by writing them down.

Some things you could write about are:

- SOMETHING YOU WISH YOU HAD SAID OR DONE
- HOW YOUR LIFE IS GOING
- HOW YOU ARE HANDLING YOUR FEELINGS
- HOW YOU ARE DOING NOW

Dear ____________________,

____

____

____

____

____

____

____

SOME OF THE GOOD THINGS I REMEMBER ABOUT MY SPECIAL PERSON ARE…

Good memories are mine to keep!

ONE OF THE IMPORTANT THINGS I LEARNED FROM THIS PERSON IS…

MY SPECIAL PERSON WILL ALWAYS LIVE IN MY HEART!

WAYS I WILL CONTINUE TO REMEMBER MY SPECIAL PERSON ARE…

American School Counselor Association (2003). *The ASCA National Model: A Framework for School Counseling Programs*. Alexandria, VA: Judy Bowers and Trish Hatch.

Bowman, R. (2005). *201 Amazing Mind Bogglers That Can be Used to Teach Kids Critical Lessons About Learning & Life*. Chapin, SC: YouthLight, Inc.

Bowman, R and Bowman, S. (1998). *Individual Counseling Activities for Children*. Chapin, SC: YouthLight, Inc.

Burnett, K. (2000). *Simon's Hook*. Roseville, California: GR Publishing.

Carr, T. (2000). *131 Creative Strategies for Reaching Children with Anger Problems*. Chapin, SC: YouthLight, Inc.

Copeland, L. (1998). *Hunter and His Amazing Remote Control*. Chapin, SC: YouthLight, Inc.

Flood, N. and Nuckols, M. (1998). *The Counseling Handbook*. Plainview, NY: Childswork Childsplay.

Frank, K. (2003). *The Handbook for Helping Kids with Anxiety and Stress*. Chapin, SC: YouthLight, Inc.

Hazbry, Nancy and Condy, Roy. (1983). *How to Get Rid of Bad Dreams*. New York, NY: Scholastic Inc.

Myrick, R. (2003). *Developmental Guidance and Counseling: A Practical Approach*, Fourth Edition. Minneapolis, MN: Educational Media Corporation.

Senn, Diane. (2004). *Small Group Counseling for Children, Grades K-2*. Chapin, SC: YouthLight, Inc.

Senn, Diane. (2003). *Small Group Counseling for Children, Grades 2-5*. Chapin, SC: YouthLight, Inc.

Shapiro, Lawrence, (1994). *Short-term Therapy with Children*. King of Prussia, Pennsylvania: The Center for Applied Psychology, Inc.

Sitsch, G. and Senn, D. (2002). *Puzzle Pieces…Classroom Guidance Connection*. Chapin, SC: YouthLight, Inc.